The World's End Murders

Tom Wood was one of Scotland's most senior and experienced operational police officers. He is an authority on crime, the policing of large-scale events and a noted authority on police perspectives on drugs and alcohol. He was appointed a Commander of the Royal Norwegian Order of Merit in 1994 and was awarded The Queen's Police Medal in 1995. Latterly he was Deputy Chief Constable and Director of Operations of Lothian and Borders Police and Officer-in-Overall Command of the linked murder investigation into the deaths of a number of young women, including Helen Scott and Christine Eadie. Since leaving the Police he has worked in the field of Alcohol and Drug Strategy and is currently Special Advisor on Early Interventions to Edinburgh's re-generation partnership.

The World's End Murders

A Thirty-year Quest for Justice

Tom Wood

David Johnston

BIRLINN

First published in 2008 by
Birlinn Limited
West Newington House
10 Newington Road
Edinburgh
EH9 1QS

www.birlinn.co.uk

ISBN13: 978 1 84158 749 3
ISBN10: 1 84158 749 4

British Library Cataloguing-in-Publication Data
A catalogue record for this book is available from the British Library

Design and typeset by Iolaire Typesetting, Newtonmore
Printed and bound by MPG Books Limited, Bodmin

Contents

Acknowledgements

The writing of this book has been a privilege and a duty, and I am grateful to the many former colleagues who encouraged and helped me in the process. I am particularly indebted to David Johnston, who has given freely of his skill and his experience in putting this book together. I am also grateful to my long serving and long suffering PA, Jeanette Shiells, who has typed, altered and altered again the various drafts and documents.

Finally, I wish to thank all my friends, past and present for all they have done to brighten my life and improve me. I would also wish to make it clear that even after receiving so much help any errors, omissions or misconceptions are entirely my own responsibility.

Tom Wood
August 2008

This book is written in memory of the young women who were victims of violent crimes in Scotland in the late 1970s, especially Christine Eadie and Helen Scott. Any proceeds due to me from its sales will be donated to Victim Support Scotland.

Tom Wood
August 2008

Introduction

As a rule I don't read policemen's memoirs. With some notable exceptions, they are usually turgid and sometimes self-seeking. I hope this is not such a memoir.

This is an account of the murder of two young women, Christine Eadie and Helen Scott, who died in October 1977. It is the story of these crimes and of the thirty-year investigation that followed.

This is not a gruesome tale of murder – the families of these young girls have suffered enough. Nor is this account devoted to the controversy in which the trial of Angus Sinclair was brought to an end in the autumn of 2007. I do not write to confront the legal profession or lay blame.

This story does, of course, have villains as any tale of murder must but it concentrates on the heroes, of whom there are many, the families of Helen and Christine who, with quiet dignity, have carried an unimaginable burden down the years and the police officers, the support staff and the scientists who, over the generations, persisted in their investigations, never gave up and, though they suffered many a setback, never forgot Helen and Christine and never let go. They number so many that it is impossible to name them all but typical among them is Detective Superintendent Ian Thomas, Detective Chief Inspector Allan Jones and Forensic Scientist Lester Knibb. With many others, these men resolutely pursued the challenges of the World's End murders over the years.

Their commitment, willpower and refusal to be defeated deserve to be remembered more than any courtroom debacle.

I have been a member of the Scottish Police Service for most of my adult life as was my father before me. This book is dedicated to all these men and women who I have been proud to work with and who have truly upheld the finest traditions of the service.

Finally, I hope the narrative paints a picture of a time and place in Scottish criminal history and refreshes the public's memory of what befell two innocent young women, Christine and Helen, as well as the others who were victims of the shocking events of 1977 and 1978.

1

The World's End

The brutal murder of two young friends on a night out in the pubs of Edinburgh's Old Town has always hung heavily on the collective mind of Scotland's capital city. The fact that the girls' killings remained under investigation for nearly thirty years took a terrible toll on their families as did the eventual collapse of the trial of the man accused of their killing. The lack of success in the long-running investigation was also the source of great frustration to the police. Over the decades, the force in which I served devoted a huge amount of time and money to trying to solve this awful crime. There had been many breakthroughs along the way and all of them petered out sooner or later but not before the hopes of everyone involved had been raised, only to be dashed again. In policing though, as in most other walks of life, perseverance pays off. So it was to do in this case. Those who persevered the hardest showed the kind of professionalism that bordered on obsession.

For many of the officers and staff involved in the World's End, the inquiry marked them and, years later, continued to intrigue them. During the final stages of the investigation, I got a number of calls from long-retired detectives anxious to know how the case had been concluded and, perhaps more importantly, whether anything they had or hadn't done had been significant.

Police forces generally pride themselves on their murder clear-up rates and we, like the general public, found it unacceptable that two young women could be abducted from our city, murdered and no one be brought to account. It may happen in other places but not in Edinburgh, not in Scotland. Now, in the twenty-first century, that may seem a strange mindset but back in the 70s it was a very strong feeling.

On a Saturday night in October 1977, two seventeen-year-old friends, Helen Scott and Christine Eadie, went for a night out in their home town of Edinburgh. The day was 15 October and it was to become a date fixed in people's minds for another reason and that would help police greatly later as we asked them to recall the events of that night many days, weeks or ever years later. It was the day after legendary American entertainer Bing Crosby died on a golf course. Events like this can often be used as signposts to point witnesses in the direction we need them to go. They may not recall one particular night on the town out of many others but they will remember the night when the radio was playing non-stop Bing Crosby and tributes to the star were being shown on TV.

Helen and Christine went to several pubs in the early part of that autumn Saturday night. They were last seen alive in a bar in the heart of the historic Old Town of Edinburgh. Various friends met up with them during the course of that evening and police were quickly able to establish a detailed picture of events – who they spoke to and what was going on in the lead-up to their disappearance. The name of that last pub they visited that night has since been inextricably linked with the killings. Even the pub's name, the World's End, has something of a macabre ring to it which seemed to add to the public horror of the events that were about to unfold. The fact the bar stands more or less exactly halfway down Edinburgh's historic Royal Mile, between the Castle at the top and the Palace of Holyroodhouse at the bottom, did nothing to detract from the crime's notoriety. It was in the nearby alleyways, known as closes, that some of Scotland's most chilling crimes were carried out.

The pub's name was passed down from the Middle Ages in the

aftermath of the Battle of Flodden in 1513 when Edinburgh was a fortified town and its walls ran close to this spot. To go out of the gates was to leave civilisation and the safety of the town. It was literally the world's end.

The Old Town provided the backdrop for the crimes of body-snatchers Burke and Hare and the notorious Deacon Brodie – figures from history whose foul deeds are recalled day in and day out by the ghost tour operators taking tourists through this ancient district. On that October night, its dark past was brought brutally up to date.

Christine and Helen had gone into the pub with some of their usual group of friends and, by all accounts, fell into the company of two men. After the girls' bodies were found, the murder inquiry traced in the region of 150 people who had been in the bar at some time or other during that night. Some of them gave evidence that seemed unimportant or minor at the time but which, thirty years later, would appear significant.

It was clear that slowly the various friends they had been with drifted off leaving Helen and Christine engrossed in conversation with these men, strangers to the usual company. No one was certain about seeing them leave – there was only one possible sighting. What was beyond doubt is that the men seen talking to the girls were not traced at the time of the original inquiry despite being the focus of intense police activity and press publicity.

The girls were never seen alive again and their bodies were found within twenty-four hours. Christine's was discovered on the fore-shore at Gosford Bay, a beautiful area of the East Lothian coastline some ten miles east of Edinburgh. She had been sexually assaulted, bound and gagged with her own tights and underwear and left naked. Helen's was found not so far away at Coates Farm, halfway between the coast and the county town of Haddington. She was partially stripped, her arms were tied with a belt and a ligature made from her own tights was round her neck. A second ligature, her belt, was also round her neck and her pants lay near her head. It was as if she had been gagged with the pants which in turn had been held in place by one of the ligatures but then she had somehow managed to spit the gag out. Many years later, the very precise way in which the bodies were left and the way in which bindings were tied and gags inserted would serve as a signpost in the final investigation. From the outset of this inquiry, officers always thought the double murder would, in all probability, have been the work of two men – not just because the girls were last seen in the company of two men but because it would have been hard for just one killer to subdue and murder two fit young people.

This simple summation of the bare facts of the case can go no way to indicate the shock that it caused – the outrage that such a cruel, vicious and depraved crime could be committed against two wholly innocent young girls out having fun on a Saturday night. This was the 1970s, a time before the general public had become somewhat hardened to violent images and the portrayal of brutal crime so common in the media today.

In 1977, I was a new boy in the CID and, uniquely, had come straight in as a sergeant, without the usual apprenticeship as a constable. I had been lucky enough to qualify for the fast-track promotion system then operating in the police. At the age of twenty-five, I was a sergeant with much to learn and with a population of highly sceptical older colleagues, many of whom had served since just after the war, as my tutors. To be on the fast track – a 'flyer' as we were always called – was both a huge benefit and a curse. In the system of that day, we were guaranteed our first rank early but nothing more. Many flyers fell by the wayside as early faux pas haunted their reputations over their entire careers. Despite this, many of us came through the ranks and did justify the confidence placed in us. By the time I left the police, many of Scotland's senior officers had come through one of the fast-track promotion systems that developed over the years. In 1977, that was small comfort to me as I found myself in at the deep end and the first-ever flyer to be posted directly to the CID.

But I did have advantages. My apprenticeship in the police had been the finest I could have asked for. After a mind-numbingly boring two-year spell as a 'points man' traffic controller in Princes Street, Edinburgh – the local traders and the Town Council resisted traffic lights till the early 70s – I was taught beat work in the Stockbridge area by a master of the art, Bob Turnbull, a man who taught me all there was to know about the proper way to work a beat as well as fly-fishing. He was to become a lifelong friend. The essence of success was simple – visibility and communication. If you worked hard at these two principles, beat work was a rewarding and successful experience but you needed to be self-reliant. There was not the numbers of fast police cars to come to your assistance as there are now. In those days, we patrolled alone at all times of the day or night.

You had to be able to look after yourself physically as well as mentally. But my first love was always crime. 'Thief catching' always fascinated me and the continual mental game of criminal detection and criminal intelligence intrigued me. Working in Stockbridge, a fairly self-contained village in these pre-yuppie days was a great place to develop these skills. The infamous brothel in a house in the smart Georgian terrace of Danube Street attracted a colourful cast of characters while the growing number of junk and antique shops serving the emerging hippy trade attracted yet another diverse group of interesting people.

Looking back I suppose my love of criminal investigation was inevitable – it ran in my blood. My father had been a long-serving detective in the 50s and my childhood memories were of the company of detectives and their tall stories, always funny and exciting to a small boy. I have no doubt that some of them were true as well.

In 1972, I got my break. After just a few years' experience, but with a good grounding in basic policing, I was posted to Drylaw which, even in the pre-heroin era, was one of the busiest police stations in Scotland, covering, as it did, the vast sprawling area of post-war housing estates of Muirhouse, Pilton and West Granton, all with high crime rates.

It is often said that experience is about concentration and not duration and, if that's true, six months at Drylaw was worth years in most other policing areas. There was a rich mix of crime to deal with in a generally very supportive community. It was there that I found out one of the great truths of policing – the rough areas, where there are real victims and where the police are needed, are where there is most support and understanding for the police. Later in my career, I was to work in communities that really didn't have a crime problem but spent much of their time bemoaning their perceived lack of security and fears.

A fairly accurate portrayal of the bleakness of life in Drylaw and Muirhouse and the devastation that heroin brought to these and many other housing schemes throughout Scotland is to be found in Irvine Welsh's novel *Trainspotting*. In the early 1970s, heroin was just emerging but, in hindsight, all the signs of the problem it would become were already there. I particularly remember how we Drylaw cops were amazed when one of the local criminals turned up with a brand-new E-type Jaguar. It was a pillar-box red convertible and it stood out like a sore thumb among the drab grey council houses. The owner was a second-rate criminal and local thug and, as we speculated on how he had managed to afford it, we never considered that he was one of the first heroin dealers in Edinburgh. In fairness, a handful of insightful drug squad detectives had been warning us about the danger of drugs and of heroin in particular but their message was heard too late to prevent what has become the curse of many of our communities and the only really significant new challenge to policing before the age of computers.

But the experience of my excellent apprenticeship was now

bearing fruit and I managed to pass the stiff selection procedures for the national accelerated promotion programme. It led to a year at the Scottish Police College where the eight of us selected that year were given intensive instruction in everything from constitutional law and management theory to public speaking. At the end of the course, I was a brand-new sergeant with everything to prove.

A brief return to Drylaw followed and then, as I realise it now, it was directly to the CID as a guinea pig. Up to then, the CID and other specialisms like the Traffic Department had been seen as forces within the force. Officers, once in the CID, seldom returned to uniform unless on promotion or punishment. The system had strengths but it also had weaknesses as it allowed the growth of cultures that could sometimes be very dangerous. The various scandals that beset the Metropolitan Police in the 1960s were a prime example of what could happen in an organisation with strong internal culture but without proper governance. The problem of corruption, either to defeat the ends of justice or for personal gain, was not prevalent in Scotland. I saw very little evidence of it throughout my career but, nonetheless, police chiefs everywhere were shaking up the CID and, in a very small way, I was part of that new regime.

So it was that, in October 1977, I was working in CID administration, keeping my head down and awaiting release as a fully fledged detective.

On the day the murders broke, there were few dealings for the new boy in the CID administrative office with the crime that was gripping the whole country but I still remember the tensions and the huge charge of energy that this crime created in the CID block of the then new force headquarters building at Fettes. There had simply not been a crime like this in our force area. I, of course, had no idea that the World's End case would run the entire length of my police career and that I would have a role to play in the final investigation.

The murders were going to be the first major challenge for the newly formed Lothian and Borders Police, just two years old at this point. It was to be a challenge that would live with the force for many more years to come.

As I detail the way this first inquiry developed, it is important to put the events I describe into the context of the times we are discussing. Certainly looking back at the newspaper cuttings of the investigation is to peer into another world. The black-and-white images carried by the *Edinburgh Evening News*, the *Scotsman* and the *Glasgow Herald* seem old-fashioned, almost antique, when viewed today. Police techniques and procedures have probably advanced more in the last thirty years than they had in the previous hundred. This was a major inquiry conducted in its initial and most crucial stages without the benefit of computers, employing scientific techniques that were limited to say the least and at a time when DNA was hardly a concept, let alone the major investigatory tool it is today.

Those were the days when senior investigators had no formal training in the investigation and management of major cases. Detectives learned as their service went along. The CID was still mainly a career within a career with some officers spending the vast majority of their time exclusively in CID with little or no interchange with other branches of the service to build a more rounded experience. The consequence of this was that the quality of CID officers was very varied. Yet, as I look back, it is remarkable how many fine natural detectives there were at all ranks. Putting aside the rose-tinted spectacles, there were some excellent investigators and leaders across the Scottish service but they were hopelessly handicapped by a lack of technology and the systematic approach now accepted as commonplace in criminal investigations.

Some things, though, change little – like the protocols and procedures for investigations that cross the boundaries of police forces or even their internal divisional areas. Police procedures then, as they do to this day, give ownership of a murder inquiry to the force or the division where the body was found – where the body lay, not where the person was last seen alive or their place of origin. This, in all truth, gave the World's End inquiry, as it became known, another large hurdle to overcome from the very outset.

Local government in Scotland, and the police service along with it, was undergoing a period of enormous change. A Royal Commission headed by the distinguished Scots judge Lord Wheatley had come up with a plan to replace the country's old burgh councils and county districts with a slimmed-down number of 'super regional authorities', each charged with running an area's major services, including the police. So it was that a series of amalgamations were enacted and a massive exercise was going on to try to harmonise working practices and end old rivalries between the newly combined eight forces.

Lothian and Borders Police was formed out of three old forces – Edinburgh City Police, Lothian and Peebles Constabulary and the Berwick, Roxburgh and Selkirk Constabulary. Each, of course, felt they had the business of policing down to a fine art and were reluctant to give up their ways for those of another force. In the west of Scotland the service was facing an even bigger challenge as seven forces worked to become one. Strathclyde police covered a massive area ranging from the tough inner-city challenges of Glasgow to the remote and beautiful islands of Argyll.

Integration is the key word in any merger, be it in the private or public sector. The people at the head of their own little empires are always reluctant, to some greater or lesser extent, to cede power or control to a new and perhaps little-known person. Nonetheless, efforts had been made to mix and match senior officers of the new forces even though practicalities made this a slow process.

These were the tensions lying behind what was going on as the investigation to find the killers of Helen and Christine was being established. The solving of crime is often dependent on what happens in the first few hours of any major inquiry. The protection of the crime scene and the fast establishment of the basic facts to allow the initial inquiries to be channelled in the right direction are vital if a solution is to be reached quickly.

The World's End inquiry was one police operation split into two from the very start. The Edinburgh end was run by a highly regarded city detective chief inspector, Bert Darling, while the East Lothian part, the main part of the inquiry because that was where the bodies had been found, was headed by Detective Chief Inspector Andrew Suddon. He was a man of equal competence but his background was in the less demanding rural force, which was much smaller in size and without many of the back-up facilities of the larger City Police. Though both men came from solid investigative backgrounds, they were very different in style and temperament. Acting as officer in overall command was Detective Superintendent George MacPherson, a tough man who had the difficult task of bringing the two teams together to act as a single unit.

Whilst the county division was nominally in charge of the direction of the inquiry, they were the least involved in the first phase to establish what had actually happened in the case of the World's End killings – the effort in those first days to find witnesses and investigate the backgrounds of the girls. It was quickly established that there were no witnesses to the dumping of the bodies, no hint of the vehicle that had to have been used. The place where Christine's body was left on the beach was yards from the roadside on a section of the route between two coastal villages. The actual piece of road where the killer's vehicle would have stopped commands a very good view of the route in both directions, allowing whoever was dumping the body to be certain that his work would not be witnessed. At night, the lights of an approaching car would be seen some distance away. Helen's body had been left in a remote field on a quiet country road nearby.

On the other hand, a great many people in the pub that night were traced and a clear picture of the girls' evening was established.

Not only were customers of the World's End traced but hundreds of people who had been drinking in the other pubs visited by the pair that night were also interviewed to see if any of them had an inkling as to who the two men they were seen with may have been. They appeared to have met the men for the first time that night in the World's End and fallen into conversation with them. Within a short space of time, both of the men were well described – to the extent that the *Edinburgh Evening News* was able, with help from the police, to print an artist's impression of the scene in the bar that night with the suspects, as they had been described by witnesses, clearly seen talking to Helen and Christine. It quickly became apparent that these men were not regulars – in fact, no one had a clue who they were. They seemed to be strangers to the Old Town area of Edinburgh, not knowingly seen by any of the pub patrons before that night. They had been observed clearly by so many people that a photofit picture of the pair was released by police in the weeks after the killings. Photofits are a mixed blessing for detectives. All too often the images created by witnesses in a genuine attempt to assist are so short of the mark that they can actually hinder the inquiry by erroneously deflecting attention elsewhere. In this case, though, we would eventually see just how accurate those photofit images actually were.

One major issue in a prolonged or high-profile murder investigation is that of public confidence. Murder, particularly multiple murders or the murder of a child, still rightly excites the public imagination. The coverage crimes such as this and the Soham and West murders get on radio, TV and in the newspapers stimulates the kind of media and public frenzy that can drive and distort the course of an investigation. However, this is not always the case. Some recent killings, like the murder of petty criminals or internecine gang murders, demonstrate that the public makes a fine judgement about the worthiness of the victim. In one recent Edinburgh case, where the victim was himself a violent criminal, the overwhelming belief that 'he had it coming' led to a poor public response and little information coming forward despite the best police and media efforts.

The very high-profile murder investigation can really be traced back to the original 1880s Whitechapel Ripper case. The unique combination of multiple and gruesome crimes with a taunting killer or killers and, crucially, an emerging tabloid press, featuring lithographs and graphic illustrations, combined to give the Ripper case a horror status that still endures today and which, at the time, must have overwhelmed the small amateur group of detectives dealing with it. Today, over a hundred years later, new theories and suspects still emerge with all the racial and class stereotypes intact – the Mad Royal, the Homicidal Foreigner and the Stranger. It's the nearest thing to the original bogey man.

Since the Whitechapel Ripper, there has been a succession of notorious cases – the Moors Murders, the Black Panther, the Yorkshire Ripper, Soham and, in Scotland, the Bible John Murders of the 1960s, the World's End case and the abduction and murders of Susan Maxwell, Caroline Hogg and Sarah Harper. All these cases, in their own way, established a place in the folk memory of the public.

The successful investigation of murder and the murder clear-up rate have always been of special importance to police forces – they are perceived as an index of proficiency and success. It is ironic when considered objectively because murder is generally not the most difficult crime to solve – the majority of killings are in a domestic situation or where the victim and offender have some degree of relationship so it is not hard to have a good murder clear-up rate. It's much more difficult to solve offences like housebreaking and robbery – crimes which also have a greater social impact because they affect a far greater number of people.

Murder, however, remains the benchmark and crimes which catch the public and media imagination place an enormous strain on the investigation team, the police force and the community. Two things are essential to maintaining public confidence – the demonstration that police are prioritising the investigation and signs that the inquiry is making progress. The importance of the investigation is frequently gauged by significant police presence, incident caravans, reconstructions or the more recent and sometimes mawkish practice of parading relatives before the media to make tearful pleas for help. The demonstration of progress and new lines of inquiry is sometimes more problematic for there is a real media pressure to come up with a new line every day and this can be both dangerous and, in the long term, counterproductive.

A number of investigations I have been involved in were distracted and sometimes misled by red herrings that had been originated by the police because they were trying, in good faith, to demonstrate their progress and satisfy an ever voracious media. Vehicle inquiries are classics of the type. In every long-running investigation, there is at least one sighting of a white van or a red car and not infrequently complicated and lengthy inquiries are made to trace them. As a senior officer, it's hard to resist the temptation of these leads. It may be crucial but very often it takes the investigation down a very long cul-de-sac. Just as importantly, features associated with the case that are misleading can also lodge in the mind of the public. This is one reason why police are always reluctant to issue photofit likenesses of suspects. If the photofit is a good likeness, that's fine but, if not, then the public is looking for someone that does not exist and that, by default, excludes everyone else.

As the World's End investigation developed, vehicle inquiries and one particular vehicle would be crucial and photofit impressions would also play an important role.

The murders of Helen and Christine were entirely different from the usual domestic killings. From an early stage, it looked as if this crime had resulted from a chance first meeting between two men and two women. It seemed likely the men had a plan to abduct a victim or victims based simply on the fact that, between the four leaving the bar that night and the bodies being found the next day, there were no sightings of them at all. There could not have been a struggle in a public place so they must have been able to persuade the pair to go with them willingly – probably in a vehicle which they knew would be safe for their evil purpose. In all likelihood, the perpetrators would have had a plan – certainly a rough idea of what they were going to do that night if they got the opportunity. One thing is striking, especially in the light of cases that came after this one. Often men seeking a victim to abduct, abuse and murder have a kit in their possession – rope for bindings and other paraphernalia. The child killer Robert Black had just such a kit in his van when he was eventually arrested. In addition to the bindings and tape for gagging his little victims, there was also a sleeping bag in which to conceal them.

The World's End killer/s got round the need to carry such items by using their victims' own clothing to suppress them – their tights became bindings, their underwear gags. So, within hours of the bodies being discovered, there were in effect two large-scale inquiries going on. There was the East Lothian-based forensic examination of the discovery sites and searches of the nearby areas to find any clues that may have been left behind and, in Edinburgh, the huge investigation focusing on the World's End pub and the city centre.

In these days of spacious modern incident rooms with air conditioning and the most up to date of computer equipment, it's easy to forget that such advances only began in the 1980s. Back in the 1970s, teams investigating murders and major incident worked out of small offices and all the data was kept on card index systems and in bulky paper files. This worked well enough for a simple domestic crime but was seriously inadequate for large or complex investigations. The manual card system dated from the 1940s and, although updated in the subsequent years, it was basically the same and it depended on the skill and experience of a small administrative team usually made up of an experienced detective sergeant and two detective constable clerks. It was the members of this small team who read the statements of witnesses and created 'jobs', the name given to further inquiries, arising from them. The senior investigator or his deputy also read the statements and might add further lines of inquiry and that was it. There were no further fail-safes, no automatic review process and no high-tech safeguards. It was a rudimentary and very basic system but it worked amazingly well and was a great testimony to the expertise of the staff who operated it. So crucial was the admin role recognised to be that senior detectives invariably had a favoured sergeant and team to work the admin of his squads – people he knew and trusted and who, above all, had the experience and track record to do the job. This arrangement established a common fund of shared experience but no unified system. The manual card index system met its nemesis on the Yorkshire Ripper inquiry in the 80s. The sheer size of that investigation swamped the manual index and culminated in a number of satellite incident rooms being crammed with tens of thousands of cards. The shortcomings were evident for, no matter how able the operators were, it was clear that the scale was beyond human capacity and, in the aftermath of the trial and conviction of Peter Sutcliffe and in the knowledge that the killer had been overlooked in the system, the Byford Report recommended a computerised major inquiry system. Thus was born HOLMES, Home Office Large Major Enquiry System, a system which, with regular modernisation, is still used today.

Back in 1977, however, two incident rooms were established and the best teams were picked to run them. In Edinburgh, one of the most experienced admin sergeants, David 'Yogi' Brunton, got the call. David, whose nickname arose from his bear-like physique, was a frontline officer with a tough exterior but he had also built a reputation for his deft handling of administration work for murder squads. This was to be his greatest test but years later, when, long after his death, his manual index was computerised, the quality of his team's work shone through.

Armed as I am now with 20/20 hindsight, it is not valid for me to criticise the steps taken in those early days but everyone in the service will agree that back then standards were very different from the ones in place today. Search techniques, for one, were rough and ready. There is no suggestion anything was missed by the officers out combing the crime scenes in 1977 but from studying the records of the time and seeing photographs of what went on, it is clear that it would be done differently today. Many years later the job of gathering of forensic evidence and its protection from contamination was done properly, giving us the basic materials we needed in later investigations.

In the city, detectives were making frequent appeals through the press for people who had visited the World's End that night to come forward even if they believed they had not seen anything relevant. Scores of them did and thankfully many of them had seen the girls. Some paid passing attention to the men who had befriended them but nothing in their behaviour in public that night would have given reason for any concern to bystanders.

Like many teenagers who had been on a night out, the girls were showing signs that they had been drinking. One part of that initial inquiry was to try to discover exactly how much each of them had drunk during the course of the evening. The significance of this was to give officers an estimate of how long after leaving the World's End they had met their deaths. A fairly accurate account of the lapse of time can be given by determining what their blood alcohol level would have been when they left the pub and what the level was in the body when it has found. A straightforward calculation can be made of the time that had elapsed by the reduction in that reading. The girls drank about the same that night but Helen's blood alcohol level was considerably lower than Christine's, suggesting quite powerfully that she had been alive rather longer than her friend.

One of the first lines of inquiry at the city end of the investigation involved the local beat officers whose patch included the World's End. In this day and age, this may sound odd but, in the 70s, the foot-beat system was still the backbone of city policing. Back then, the constables knew their beats and they took pride in their ownership of a particular patch and felt a very real responsibility for it. There was a system of day and night foot beats across the city centre while, on the outskirts, panda cars operated a system much more like the one we have today. In the centre, however, the beats were still based on a 1930s system which used police boxes, flashing beacons and lines of sight – a method of working that had been in existence long before portable radios became the norm. The day beats were usually fairly big and divided into hourly and half-hourly turns. Each turn would have a very detailed route of patrol that made sure the whole area was regularly policed and, in the days before radio when policemen patrolled alone, this meant that they could be found and supervised by their sergeant. During the night, the system was different in the city centre as each nightshift officer would only have a very small area to patrol so that they could check the security of property, provide a constant visible street presence and be on hand to supervise the emptying of the pubs and clubs. Because of this, the chances were that, when Helen and Christine left the World's End late on 15 October, a police officer would have been near at hand and this indeed proved to be the case.

Coincidentally one of the very young policemen working in the vicinity of the High Street that night was Malcolm Dickson. Later, as an assistant chief constable and assistant inspector of constabulary, he would become a close colleague and friend of mine. We often discussed that night and, although he saw nothing of significance himself, neither he nor any of the officers on duty that night ever forgot 15 October 1977. In fact, the beat men who were patrolling outside the World's End gave valuable information to the inquiry team for they had seen two girls like Helen and Christine that night – in the company of two men – it was a small step but an important one. The two men had appeared to be hanging around outside the World's End but not in a threatening kind of way. Two police officers, casually observing closing time in the High Street, spoke of how it seemed that the men were trying to engage with the girls. Those sightings were probably the last time Helen and Christine were seen alive.

It is extraordinarily difficult for the senior officers in charge of a large inquiry like this to keep control of all aspects of the case and monitor with exact precision the various directions in which it is going. It remains difficult to this day but would have been even more so in 1977 when, without computers, there was a huge reliance on the recollections of individual officers and the primitive card index systems to try to ensure the key threads of the investigation were identified.

There is huge pressure on them from both within and outside the police service to come up with results and to do so quickly. The danger always is that, in the absence of any clear leads and direct evidence, it is too easy to be distracted by hunches and suspicions not born of hard evidence or to be led astray to pursue inquiries that do not justify a priority. In a recent example, the hunt for the so-called Washington sniper was predicated on the fact that he drove a white van to the scenes of his shootings. This threw a cloud of suspicion over every white van man in the DC area. Of course it was later discovered that the presence of the van was coincidental and the sniper drove no such vehicle. Decisions have to be taken when weighing up the quality of evidence and which lines of inquiry are to be pursued. It would be possible to start tracing the owners and drivers of all white vans in order to eliminate the innocent. But it's easy to see just how quickly this could engulf the whole inquiry and ultimately a sizeable part of the nation's police service.

The World's End

The World's End had something of a white van lead, only it was slightly more manageable. All the descriptions of the two men given by the various witnesses agreed on the fact that one of them had short cropped hair – a soldier's haircut. This man was also said to be of very smart appearance which added to the impression that he could have a military background. The Royal Mile was popular with off-duty soldiers from the various barracks in and around Edinburgh and the view was taken that the man with the short hair may well have been in the army. So it was that, early in the investigation, a substantial part of the inquiry team's manpower was devoted to speaking to soldiers based at Dreghorn, Glencorse and the other camps near the capital who had been out that Saturday night. The soldier scenario was an appealing one. It could explain why the pair were strangers in the pub on a Saturday night and, such is the transient nature of life in the army, they could be well out of the area by the time the murder inquiry was underway. Naturally, checking out this possibility was a demanding task. The fact the events under examination had taken place late on a Saturday evening did not help the recollections of many of the young soldiers being interviewed.

Christine Eadie's body had been found first and Helen Scott's just a few hours later. All of Christine's outer clothing had been removed and, to this day, has never been found. She had been bound and gagged in a very precise fashion. Helen's body was partially stripped and she had been bound and gagged in an almost identical manner. There was extensive forensic evidence to be gathered from both bodies and also body fluids from the attacker or attackers. DNA profiling had not been discovered in those days so there were no leads there but fate intervened in those first hours in a way that eventually contributed significantly to the investigation. One of the forensic team at the scene was a young South African by the name of Lester Knibb who remained with the Lothian and Borders force for the rest of his career. Lester personally saw to the care and preservation of the evidence from the crime scenes for many years. This meant that, when DNA testing was developed as an investigatory tool, we had the samples retained in a professional manner, with their legal integrity intact and ready to form the very core of the case that would eventually be brought to court.

The various leads that came up from the interviews with soldiers, friends of the girls and other witnesses were pursued with vigour but, despite the commitment of the officers directly involved and the huge manpower deployed, the World's End inquiry was soon running out of steam. As well as the many red herrings, there were also the false witnesses, ranging from fantasists to clairvoyants, who tend to be drawn to major police investigations of this kind. This category includes people so fascinated or horrified by events that they imagine themselves to have key roles in the drama.

One case in particular highlights this phenomenon. I was a detective inspector involved in the investigation of the abduction of five-year-old Caroline Hogg from the promenade at Portobello, a seaside area of Edinburgh. Her disappearance, coming as it did just a short time after the abduction and murder of another little girl, Susan Maxwell in the Borders, turned into one of those missing person inquiries that instantly had all the resources of our force thrown at it. I became fascinated by the emergence of a number of witnesses who, on the face of it, seemed perfectly credible and who had been in the area that day. They had become so overcome with grief and the emotion of the whole case – Caroline was missing for a considerable period of time before her body was found – that some imagined themselves into positions of importance in the investigation. They amassed substantial knowledge of the events surrounding this little girl's disappearance by avidly reading every newspaper article and soaking up the details of the case. Such was the volume of knowledge that these false witnesses built up, they could appear to be central to events until they had been subjected to time-consuming interviews. Sometimes these people are deluded through mental illness and sometimes they cannot be characterised as liars or fakes because they are well-motivated people who actually believe what they have imagined to be true. Whatever category they fall into, these people are extremely dangerous to an investigation that is desperate for new leads and lines of inquiry. They can be difficult to deal with and can tie up huge amounts of manpower as officers try to get to the bottom of false stories. And, worst of all, they can lead the investigation down a completely wrong track.

In the World's End case, avenues of inquiry turned into dead ends and information dried up. The teams were slowly wound down as their work came to an end and, within the relatively short time of about seven months, it was decided there was insufficient prospect of a breakthrough to continue to devote large resources to the investigation. The massive card indexes were boxed up and the inquiry was put on a care and maintenance basis but the public pressure on the police to solve this case did not let up. It was added to over the following months by the murder of a young woman called Agnes Cooney in Glasgow on 2 December of that year. It was not long before the press were linking the World's End murders directly with that of Agnes Cooney and two other girls who had been murdered in the west not long before Helen and Christine died. They were Anna Kenny, who had disappeared and was feared killed in August 1977, and Hilda McAuley, who had been killed just thirteen days before the World's End murders.

Whilst the press were quick to ask whether the killings could be connected, the police were anxious to play down any possibility that the cases were linked. In hindsight, it seems a strange course of action for murders with such apparent similarities not to be investigated together or at least for them to be the subject of enhanced cooperation and liaison between the forces involved. Equally one can understand the reluctance of officers to create what would undoubtedly have become widespread public alarm until such time as they could be absolutely certain the five had all met their deaths at the hands of the same killer or killers.

Strathclyde police were facing the same challenges as Lothian and Borders as they struggled to amalgamate smaller forces into one cohesive organisation. Officers in the west of Scotland were faring little better with their three cases than we in the east were doing with ours and soon all the various inquiries had run out of new leads and, one by one, the investigations were slowly being wound down.

Just how unacceptable it would have been to the public and politicians for a line to be drawn under these inquiries if it was generally thought all five murders were by the same hand is clear to see. However, the fact is that, if an inquiry is exhausted, no amount of goodwill or pressure will rekindle it without new information to go on. Over the next few years, in the case of the World's End murders, senior officers who had been uncon-nected to the original inquiry carried out thorough reviews of the evidence and the investigations to date generally. These inevitably concluded that everything that could have been done had been done and there was no new information important enough to justify reopening the case.

Such was the desire within Lothian and Borders Police to solve the World's End murders that, whilst the case may have spent long periods of time not as an active inquiry, it was never a forgotten one. A senior officer within the force CID was always responsible for monitoring the investigation and was required to be aware of possible connections or new breakthroughs. Briefed by those who went before them and ever eager to find a good reason to reopen inquiries, many detectives on their way up through the ranks of the force were given responsibility for the case. Typically the case spent long periods seeing little, if any, activity and then some event would happen – some breakthrough or arrest of a potential suspect be made known – and it was up and running again.

On down the years, the World's End was never a dead case. For close on thirty years, it was truly 'under investigation'.

2

Helen and Christine

Victims of crime, and sadly in the case of the World's End their bereaved family and friends, invariably ask themselves one question which goes right to the heart of their emotions. Did they do anything to make themselves vulnerable? In simple terms the answer always has to be no – offending is always the responsibility of the offender. 'Did they act in a reckless fashion to put themselves more at risk?' is sometimes a tougher question. There is no doubt that, in some cases, people do make themselves vulnerable by being in the wrong place at the wrong time or, more likely, being in a condition where they cannot look after themselves. This is not to justify or to excuse the perpetrator – it is just plain common sense. We all have the responsibility to take reasonable care of ourselves.

In recent times, this area has become sensitive as heavy drinking among young women becomes more common and allegations of sexual assault and rape rise. While some women's groups take strong exception to this view, the connection is inescapable. The fact is that, if a woman is drunk, she is less able to protect herself and is more likely to fall victim. This is not a moral position and it is not right – it is simply a fact and one of the reasons we urgently need to think carefully about our relationship with alcohol and other substances that can increase vulnerability, as well as damage our health.

In the World's End case, however, this was not a major factor.

Helen and Christine

Helen and Christine had enjoyed an evening out. They had been drinking but this probably didn't contribute in any significant way to their fate. I believe they simply had the tragic misfortune to meet two of the most evil and predatory people that have walked the streets of our nation in modern times. They created their own downfall no more that the slowest of the herd falls victim to a predator on the African plains. When the perpetrators of these crimes walked into their hunting ground, be it in a pub or a disco or a dance hall, I believe, from the very moment they crossed the threshold, they would be callously weighing up the potential of all the young women in the room. They would be looking for the girl or girls that would fit their bill. They had probably unconsciously created a target profile in their own minds of who would make an ideal victim. They would quickly dismiss those who presented problems that could stand in the way of their intended control and violent sexual gratification.

Casting an eye round the room, they would instantly exclude the female halves of obvious couples. Out too would be the quiet group of young women who were deep in conversation. The picture soon becomes clear. The target would be girls in high spirits, the ones who have had a drink or two which leads to their guard being lowered – in fact, the sort of girls you see every night of the week in pubs and clubs in every part of the country. Normally, girls on a night out owe their safe return home at the end of these evenings to the simple fact that they did not have the misfortune to bump into a predatory criminal before their front door closes with them safely on the inside.

Helen Scott and Christine Eadie had known each other since their first days at secondary school. Helen, the older of the two by a matter of five months, and Christine met up at Edinburgh's Firrhill High School in the Oxgangs area of the city. The 1960s buildings housed a school of about 1,000 pupils. The pair had spent their entire secondary school life there and, even as seventeen-year-olds who had been out in the world of work for some time, many of their regular friends hailed from that area and Firrhill School.

The school then, as now, serves a close-knit, largely working-class community. The area was quite different from the quiet beauty of the Scottish Borders where Helen spent the first part of her life. Her mum Margaret had moved from the Edinburgh area to Coldstream on the banks of the river Tweed in the late 1950s. The epitome of a quiet town, Coldstream is famed as the place where, in 1660, General Monck raised his Regiment of Foot and marched them to London. Once in the capital, Monck helped to secure the restoration the Stuart monarchy. Coldstream is bordered by the estate of the Earls of Home, the most famous of whom was the Tory Prime Minister Sir Alec Douglas-Home. It is also a town that has been touched by tragedy. Just a few miles away is Flodden Field, the scene of the battle in 1513 that saw the flower of Scots nobility cut down by the English. And, a few years after Helen's death, it was the centre of an inquiry into the disappearance of little Susan Maxwell who was subsequently found to have been murdered by that monster of Scottish criminal history, the child-killing van driver Robert Black.

Margaret met and married Morian Scott and, a year later, Helen was born. Helen had two older half-sisters, and eventually the family would be completed with the birth of her brother Kevin. By the time Kevin was born, the family had moved to Penicuik, a dormitory town to the south of Scotland's capital. The family's final move was into the suburbs of Edinburgh after Helen's dad started a new job as a British Telecom engineer. Their home was on the strangely named Swan Spring Avenue. This street of relatively new houses in the Comiston district takes its name from the very first piped water supply to Edinburgh. There were a number of natural springs in the area that were tapped to provide supplies to the rapidly growing population and each outlet was marked by a stone carved with the figure of a bird or animal. As well as Swan Spring, there were Hare, Fox and Peewit Springs.

Helen was part of a close and loving family. At school, she had been quite quiet at first, a little reserved, but eventually her bright personality had come to the fore and she was a pupil who was well liked by staff and students alike. She left Firrhill at the age of fifteen and, just like many of her age group, she was mainly interested in fashion, music and going to the cinema. When she left school, her closest friend was a girl called Jacqueline Inglis. She remained friends with Jacquie to the end. Jacquie was with Helen in the World's End the night she disappeared and was therefore one of the last people who knew her to see the teenager alive.

Helen had worked hard since leaving school and was never out of a job. At the time of her murder, she had recently started a new job at a kilt shop in Edinburgh's main shopping thoroughfare, Princes Street. Everything was going well for her. She had a stable group of friends and a determination to improve herself which was evidenced by a recent decision to start night classes with the aim of passing Higher English and Maths. It seemed she saw her job in the kilt shop as a temporary one while she set about getting the qualifications she would need to pursue a career in what seems to have been her chosen occupation of childcare. She had already demonstrated her aptitude for this by becoming the favoured babysitter for her sister's two children.

Like many girls in their mid teens, Helen's weekend fun centred on her newly found ability to get into Edinburgh pubs and clubs with a group of friends that remained fairly constant despite the fact that they were underage. Their regular haunt was a bar called the Spider's Web in Morrison Street in the city centre.

Helen's last night began in the usual sort of way. She had arranged to meet her close friend Jacquie Inglis at Jenners' corner on Princes Street. The landmark store in the heart of the city centre is often referred to as the Harrods of the North and is a regular starting point for people meeting up for a night out in Edinburgh. The pair walked through the fading autumn light to the Mount Royal Hotel which overlooks the valley of Princes Street Gardens, lying between Edinburgh's Old and New Towns.

After a drink at the Mount Royal, the girls began to head for their next rendezvous in the High Street, the central part of the famous Royal Mile. Their journey that night took them over Waverley Bridge and, from there, it was a long steep climb up Cockburn Street to the High Street. Helen and Jacquie were heading for the Royal Mile Centre and the Wee Windaes pub where they had arranged to meet Christine Eadie and a newer member of their group, a young woman called Toni Kivlin. She was somewhat older than the rest of the girls but they enjoyed her company and she fitted in well.

Detailed examination of the statements provided by many of the people present that night showed clearly that, by the time the four met up at about eight o'clock, they had all had a drink or two. More was soon on the way as the party of four proceeded to make short visits to several other pubs in the area. There had been a typical teenage disagreement at one point – just a slight falling-out. Christine was becoming irritated by Helen's light-hearted behaviour and told her to stop acting stupidly and a bit of an argument ensued. There had been a minor fuss too when Toni Kivlin went to the toilet in one of the pubs only to emerge seconds later in something of a panic, saying she couldn't stand the sight of blood. It seems Helen had suffered a nosebleed. It didn't amount to much and soon they were off again, eventually walking into the World's End pub at just after ten o'clock.

During the new investigation I read in detail the statements given by Christine and Helen's friends at the time of the original inquiry and it was striking just how ordinary a night out it was for this group of teenage friends. The little dramas played out that evening are just the same as those played out in every town centre across the country every weekend but, in this case, the knowledge of how the night was to end could only add considerable poignancy to these descriptions of innocent, everyday events.

Helen and Christine started drinking whisky at the World's End and they squeezed into a space near the payphone in the busy bar. Just how busy it was that night was shown to the wider public by a striking artist's impression of the scene printed in the *Edinburgh Evening News* in an attempt to help what had become a double murder investigation. There were of course no mobile phones in those days but, then as now, teenagers love to talk on the phone and first Helen and then Toni were chatting to pals on the bar payphone. It was clear from the statements given by people in the pub that drink was beginning to play a large part in how this group behaved. Helen came off the phone at one point after speaking to a young male friend of hers in Coldstream where she still had strong connections. She took exception to a comment Christine made about having to phone the boy in a call box in the Borders town because he didn't have a telephone at home. Helen had walked out of the pub only to be brought back in by a peacemaker from the group sent outside to fetch her.

So it went on. The girls managed to get a seat at a table and soon other friends had joined them. They were now a large group who were engaged in animated conversation. Everybody knew one another – they were a regular crowd who met up most weekends. Boys and girls, they were all around the same age and, in some cases, they had been friends for years. Christine and Helen had obviously put their differences aside and were as usual at the heart of the crowd. To the others, it was very noticeable that they were happy and smiling. Like many true friends, there could be a disagreement one minute which would be forgotten the next and life goes on.

It was at this point, unbeknown of course to any of this group, that things were about to go wrong. Jacquie Inglis and Toni Kivlin went to the toilet together and emerged a short time later to find that Helen and Christine had been joined by two men. No one can be certain but it seems entirely likely that the pair standing in the crowded bar talking to the tipsy teenagers were embarking on a carefully laid plan that would lead to the rape and murder of these two innocent girls. If this belief is indeed correct, it gives a first chilling insight into the character of the men who had the nerve to engage the girls in conversation and quickly befriend them knowing, as I am sure they must have done, that their intention was assault, rape and murder. The men would probably have been watching the group before deciding to move in on Helen and Christine and begin the process of ensnaring them. And, what's more, they'd have been perfectly aware that the girls had friends in the pub who could easily return to be in their company, giving the friends a greater chance of being able to identify or at least describe the two men chatting to Helen and Christine. Such behaviour demonstrates a coolness, a determination and a total disregard for life if that life stood between them and their gratification.

Jacquie was later to tell officers that the men appeared to be in fairly intense conversation with Helen and Christine. They appeared unremarkable and certainly gave no one any cause for alarm. One was in his late twenties, of medium height and quite stocky. Jacquie Inglis noticed he had piercing brown eyes. His round face had prominent cheekbones and was topped by parted dark hair that lay across his forehead. His flared brown-and-white striped trousers, brown V-neck jersey and light-coloured shirt were the fashion of the day. The second man was about the same age but slightly taller. He too was wearing the flared trousers that were so popular in the late 70s. Jacquie left the four of them to get on with it and began chatting to another friend who invited them all to go to a party that was going to start quite shortly. She asked Helen and Christine if they wanted to go too. In what was to be a fateful decision, Christine said a definite no and Helen didn't appear to reply. The conversation with the two men was obviously more engaging. One of the men was leaning over the table and then walked to the bar where Jacquie thought he bought the girls a whisky each. It was the last moment she saw her friends alive. Just a few moments after witnessing this scene, the group going to the party left the pub. In the event, I suppose, like so many of these things, the party they went to fell short of expectations and Toni and Jacquie left in the early hours of the next morning to go to their respective homes by taxi – the end to just another Saturday night out.

It was 10.30 on Sunday morning when Jacquie got the first clue that something was wrong. Helen's dad Morian phoned her to see if his daughter had stayed the night with her. Later that day, a slightly concerned Jacquie went round to the flat where Christine was living, only to discover there was no sign of her or Helen. She went to a telephone box to tell her missing friend's dad. After more phoning round, Jacquie met up with some of their friends from the night before in another High Street pub. They were joined by Morian and Margaret Scott who, by this time, were extremely worried. The group decided it was best to report Helen and Christine missing. The mystery of their disappearance was not to last for long. Shortly after her visit to the South Side police station in Edinburgh to make the missing person's report, Jacquie heard a newsflash on the radio saying the bodies of two girls had been found. She immediately phoned the police and a detective came straight to her house to take a statement. The officer had the painful task of confirming that Jacquie's worst fears had been realised and that, pending formal identification, it was indeed her friends who had been found dead in East Lothian.

The subsequent murder investigation was going to need comprehensive profiles of both victims so officers spent considerable time unearthing the details of Helen and Christine's short lives. In an inquiry like this, no aspect can ever be dismissed as too small. Most murder victims are known to the killers so the first step in nearly every murder inquiry is to establish who the friends and acquaintances of the deceased were and who they were last with.

Christine had been largely brought up by her maternal grand-mother in a loving and generous family. No doubt she threw up the challenges of many teenagers but it was clear that, by the time she had reached the age of seventeen, she was an attractive, confident and outgoing young woman with an appetite for life. After she was killed, officers found a diary in Christine's flat. In it were extensive accounts of her life and experiences but none of the details yielded any clues to her killer's identity.

On leaving school, Christine had worked for a time in the city council's Education Department before taking up a post as a typist with a firm of surveyors in Edinburgh.

The information about the girls given here and heard in court during the trial serves to reinforce one simple but very important fact – something that can get buried as a crime is described and discussed in newspapers and amongst professionals working in the various fields involved. So it is worth pausing for a moment to remember that all crimes involve real people – relatives and friends who, often through no fault of their own, find their lives devastated by sheer evil and inhumanity. In the case of the World's End murders, it was not just the dead girls who were affected. It is their family and friends – the parents who live with the agony of loss every single day of the rest of their lives and the brothers and sisters who never get over the tragedy and the loss of their sisters' futures. Had their lives not been snuffed out thirty years ago, Helen and Christine may have been mothers and even grandmothers today. Who knows how many future lives and opportunities were ended that night in October 1977? As I became more acquainted with the details of the World's End inquiries and those of the other murdered victims that eventually were linked to the investigation, the suffering of those left behind screamed out of the files and reports that crossed my desk.

It is a sad fact that many of the relatives of murder victims never recover from their grief. Some die prematurely and are often said by those who survive them to have succumbed to a broken heart. Unable to cope with the grief, some take their own lives and, in their despair, others turn to the bottle in the hope of finding some kind of solace. Yet, in the cruellest of ironies, it is usually the murderers, the infamous, who are remembered by the public. Sadly, notoriety sometimes brings with it a form of immortality.

One of the biggest changes I have seen in my police career is the recognition of this fact and a realisation by the service as a whole that more has to be done to help the victims of crime and those affected by it. This is one of the prime motivations in my decision to write this book and give my royalties from it to the charity Victim Support Scotland, whose work I have seen at first hand and come to admire. It is right to say, however, that as the 2003 investigation into the events all those years ago began, we found ourselves reaping the harvest of old police attitudes.

Until the last ten to twenty years, the difficulties facing those affected by crime were all too often ignored or treated lightly by the investigators. this was because of a number of reasons. The main one was, of course, cultural. Police attitudes change as those of the rest of society do and, in the old days, victims of crime could be seen as something of a nuisance – a hindrance to the effective investigation and detection of criminals. All too often, they were seen as simply a source of information and not fully appreciated as human beings in their own right – human beings who were often going through the worst and most devastating experience of their lives.

In hindsight, of course, this was short-sighted. Families of victims can be of immense practical assistance to the investigation. They usually only seek courtesy, respect and information and, while there was a traditional reluctance to share any information in a difficult investigation for fear that it might be leaked to the press, this fear was usually misplaced. In many years of investigation, I can think of hardly any families who have betrayed the trust of the investigators and, in the thirty years since the tragic loss of their girls, the families of Helen and Christine have behaved with the utmost dignity. In the most nightmarish circumstances and in the long glare of publicity, the Scott and Eadie families have carried themselves with great courage. They have always supported the police investigations and, over the years, have gained the utmost respect and admiration of all the investigators.

But this isn't always the case. Not all relationships between the police and the families of victims are as good as those the police shared with the Scott and Eadie families. Sometimes tensions between families and police arise – for example, if people feel they are being starved of information or just not given the courtesy and respect they deserve. Cases from different parts of Scotland that could potentially be linked to the deaths of Helen and Christine were identified so it was decided that a joint operation, to be known as 'Operation Trinity', would be set up to coordinate them. When the deaths of their loved ones were initially investigated, there had been some tension between certain members of the families and the police so one of the priorities for officers working on Trinity was to establish good relationships with surviving family members from the outset. In line with modern police practice, family liaison officers were appointed and it was up to them to try to ensure that they rebuilt any broken bridges that the passage of time had done little to mend.

Of course in the last ten years the importance of family liaison has been recognised and is now a specialist area of policing with carefully selected officers receiving training to help in this, their most difficult and sensitive role. To get close to, to almost be part of, a family in grief is to share that grief. To follow the case and take the families through from crime to investigation to trial and beyond can be extremely demanding. The role of family liaison officer is not for everyone and the long-term effects can be stressful, even life changing. I know of several colleagues who have been permanently marked by difficult or harrowing cases. In the sometimes tough world of the officers serving in murder squads, family liaison is sometimes seen as a soft job, a secondary consideration. Experienced officers or those who have done the job themselves know different.

The family liaison officers – FLOs – in our investigation did a fine job. I hope the work they have done in the twenty-first century has gone some way to redress the hurt that must sometimes have been caused through lack of sensitivity in the policing ways of the last century.

As I have said, in the World's End case, perhaps because of circumstances, perhaps because of other factors, Helen Scott and Christine Eadie's families had a good working relationship with the police throughout these long and difficult years. Because of the dedication of the officers, over the years, as new initiatives were tried, the family members were amongst the first to be kept informed about what was happening. That made part of the inquiry slightly easier. It should always be remembered that, for many victims and their families, the shock, hurt and pain of crime does not disappear – it simply matures and, like a disfigurement, is constantly present.

Helen's mother Margaret died in her mid sixties and her surviving relatives were certain that the burden of grief over her murdered daughter played a significant part in her early death. And, by the time we were making progress towards our eventual breakthrough, Christine's gran, who had played such a large part in her upbringing, was also dead but her mum Margaret and Helen's dad Morian were very much alive. Both were briefed regularly as we tried to ensure they knew of each development before reading about it in the newspapers.

The first inquiry into the World's End murders had failed, of course, to identify the two men who were seen talking to the girls. It had also failed to uncover any hard evidence of whether the men had left in the company of the girls. The nearest that was unearthed was the statement of two police officers on duty in the High Street that night and who, by coincidence, were in the street near the bar at about the time Helen and Christine are thought to have left.

Beat constables John Rafferty and George Owenson were on the usual Saturday night detail in the centre of Edinburgh around closing time. As folk were piling out on to the streets at about 11.15, the officers were no doubt keeping a relaxed but wary eye on proceedings, trying to spot where any trouble might be likely to start so that they could stop it before it got out of hand.

We do not know for certain but it is likely that, since the pair were on patrol in the High Street, they could well have been close to the main door of the World's End around the time the girls and their killers were coming out of the pub and, indeed, may even have seen the four of them. Of course they had no reason to intervene – it was just another Saturday night, just another crowd of people ranging from merry to downright drunk spilling out on to the pavement.

The High Street then, as indeed now, is always rather gloomy at night. The high buildings and numerous alleyways and side streets mean street lighting is never terribly effective but the officers clearly saw two girls and two men leaving together. They saw one of the girls trip. The other girl helped her friend back on to her feet and PC Rafferty recalled they appeared to be bickering about how they were going to get home. He saw what he described as a youth approach them and offer a lift. A second 'youth' was on hand. In what perhaps was the fateful moment one girl accepted the lift, the other seemed reluctant but was nevertheless dragged off by her friend down St Mary's Street. The officers saw them disappear down the street and thought nothing more of it that night.

As I say, we can't be sure it was Helen and Christine the PCs had seen – they were unable to confirm the girls' identities despite studying a number of family photographs. Also, because of the everyday nature of what they saw, they had no clear recollection of the two men except that one of them spoke with what Rafferty said was a country accent. If that was Christine and Helen, it was the last anyone, other then their killers, saw of them alive. The next anyone was to know of the two friends was less than twenty-four hours later. First to be found was Christine.

Derek Taylor and his wife Ruth took advantage of a late autumn sunny Sunday to drive down to East Lothian from their Edinburgh home. They stopped in a sand dune car park near the East Lothian village of Longniddry and had a picnic lunch before taking a stroll along the beach. This is a scenic stretch of coast and, looking out to sea to the left, it boasts views across the Firth of Forth to Fife. You can also see Edinburgh's waterfront stretching out some ten miles to the west. To the south is Gosford House, the stately home of the Earl of Wemyss and March.

After half an hour's walking, the imposing entrance to the grounds of Gosford House, on their right-hand side, came into view. Then, to their left, Mr Taylor spotted what he thought was a tailor's dummy lying by the high-water mark. Inquisitive, he walked across and, as he got closer, he was horrified to realise it was no dummy. It was a naked girl lying supine and, when he reached the spot, he could see she had a gag in her mouth.

Quickly he ran to the lodge house of the nearby estate and called the police. Christine had not been reported missing at this time and so, when officers arrived at the scene, there was nothing to help them with the identity of the body that lay before them.

A similar drama would take place a few miles away later that afternoon. By that time, it was becoming clear to the police that they were dealing with a major investigation of a double murder involving the girls who by this time had been reported missing.

Not far inland from Gosford lies Coates Farm. It is situated on a picturesque back road that could be taken by someone wanting a leisurely drive from Longniddry to the county town of Haddington.

John MacKenzie worked as a gardener at a nearby house and, as usual, he had left his cottage in the grounds early that evening to take his dog for a walk down the road towards Coates. He too thought the object he saw lying in a field was a tailor's dummy. He did not venture into the stubble field but as he peered through the gathering gloom he, like Derek Taylor, came to the sudden and awful realisation that it was a woman's body. He could clearly see her hands were tied behind her back. She had no shoes on and her legs were bare but a black coat was on the upper part of her body. Shocked to the core Mr MacKenzie ran home and drove to Haddington police office to report what he had seen.

By this time, the East Lothian division of the force would have been buzzing. As the full realisation of what they were dealing with became apparent to the senior officers on duty, the usual Sunday afternoon skeleton staff was quickly boosted by people brought in from rest days.

3

The First Investigation

The initial investigation into the double killing ran at full tilt from the moment the bodies were found in mid October 1977 until the end of May the following year.

There were several main lines of inquiry being followed up under the various teams controlled by Detective Superintendent MacPherson, with DCIs Darling and Suddon commanding the two strands of the investigation, one based in East Lothian and the other based in the capital.

Tracing and eliminating patrons of the World's End pub on the night the girls vanished was of prime importance and, given the fact that most murders are committed by people who know or have met their victims, it was a channel of investigation that looked hopeful. But it was more difficult than it first seemed. The World's End was then, as it is now, a busy pub and, being on the tourist route, it has always attracted both regulars and casual customers who pass down the Royal Mile, pop in for a drink and move on. It was no different in the 70s and, on a Saturday night, the pub was full of a mixture of people, some who stayed for the evening, most who called in, had a drink, checked out the action – the girls, the boys – and moved on up the Mile.

Trying to fully establish who was in the pub and when was a tricky exercise. Add to that the difficulty of cross-referring very different descriptions of the same people and you can start to understand the complexity. If the World's End killings had taken place in 2007 not 1977, there would have been a wealth of technical information to assist the inquiry team. The CCTV footage from the numerous cameras both within the pub and in the streets nearby would have been immensely valuable. The credit card details of customers who either paid by credit card in the vicinity or drew cash from nearby cash machines would be retrieved and followed up. Any vehicles checked on the Police National Computer or picked up on the various cameras in and around the city would be traced. Mobile telephone activity in the vicinity could even be scrutinised. Back in 1977, these technologies did not exist. We could not even establish who had used the payphone in the pub that night. The detectives back then had to log timelines and people's positions on a huge paper chart much as detectives had done a hundred years before. Yet, as we looked back thirty years later, we were amazed just how accurate a job they did and how good some of the descriptions given had been.

At the centre of the pub inquiry were, of course, the two men who had been seen chatting to Helen and Christine and who were believed to have left the pub with them.

There are simple first priorities in homicide investigations, secure the locus, identify the body, establish the cause of death and trace who was the last person to see the victim alive. The two men seen with Helen and Christine in the pub and who apparently left with them were a natural priority. Not that it was a foregone conclusion that they were the culprits – all sorts of things could have happened between the door of the World's End and Gosford Beach. Nor could the failure of these two men to come forward be taken as a definite sign of guilt. There could have been a number of reasons why they had not come forward. They may not have known of the incident – though, given the massive publicity, this was unlikely. It is more likely that they should not have been there in the first place – they could have been married and being seen chatting to young girls in a pub would have meant they'd have some explaining to do.

There are many reasons why vital witnesses are sometimes reluctant to come forward and it is an age-old problem for the police to coax them to do so. As it transpired, the original inquiry team never traced the two men in the pub with Helen and Christine.

The next problem for the original investigators was to sort out, evaluate and prioritise the mass of information, suggestions and names that came forward in the first weeks after Helen and Christine's murder. There was a genuine mood of public outrage, fanned by an active and imaginative media. There was a sense that this crime, above all others, was beyond belief – it couldn't happen in Edinburgh, it was the stuff of American cop fiction not reality – and the shock waves rebounded for many weeks. Frequently women who were in their teens in the late 70s tell me of the impact of the World's End killings. They were subjected to parental clampdowns on late nights in the town, the importance of staying with the group was emphasised and, in the pre-mobile phone era, they were encouraged to keep in touch while they were out and about. Taxis did a roaring trade and many a father stayed up to the small hours to make sure a daughter came home safely. That year saw a tangible death of innocence in Edinburgh and the enormous groundswell of emotion led to thousands of pieces of information coming to the hard pressed incident rooms.

High-profile cases produce an interesting mix of responses. Genuine witnesses come forward but so do well-motivated ones whose information is irrelevant. Attention seekers appear as do those with a morbid fascination for the crime. And then there are the ones with malicious intentions, eager to settle a score or do a bad turn to an enemy. Add to that the deranged, the mediums and those so caught up in the event that they imagine themselves being in key witness roles and you start to get a picture of an incident room in the first few weeks of a major and high-profile inquiry. In 1977, the media intervention had not reached the twenty-four-hour frenzy we saw during the Soham and Madeleine McCann cases but, even so, this was a dangerous time for senior investigators. It is very easy to be drawn up one of the many blind alleys that always await the unwary.

It is clear that George MacPherson, Bert Darling and Andrew Suddon kept cool heads for the documents from 1977 clearly indicate their focus and determination not to be distracted. The main lines of inquiry remained on the patrons of the World's End, the two men and the East Lothian connection. Those close to Helen and Christine, the local boys in their group of friends, were quickly eliminated. Legitimate major lines of inquiry did, however, emerge. Near to where the bodies had been left is the caravan site at Port Seton. Then, as now, this holiday camp attracted many visitors from the West of Scotland. It was largely closed in October when the girls were murdered but those who frequented it in the summer, perhaps owned caravans there, would know the area and the back roads and might have access to the site even while closed.

A larger and more complex line of inquiry was also emerging in Edinburgh. Naturally the two men last seen with Helen and Christine were described differently by different witnesses but all agreed they were smart with short hair. In the late 70s, this was not typical for young men – long hair and straggly moustaches were still the rage – so it was logical that the minds of the inquiry team focused on the military garrison at Edinburgh Castle, then an operational army base as well as a ceremonial HQ. Young soldiers were regular customers in the High Street pubs – they were smartly dressed and, of course, all had the standard army short back and sides. Given the information available at the time, it was a line of inquiry that had to be pursued but it was hugely problematic and it took considerable time and resources to tackle.

Years later, my good friend Dougie Kerr, who retired as a chief superintendent but who had been a young detective on the original squad, told me how challenging the 'soldier' side of the inquiry had been. Like most barracks, Edinburgh Castle saw a constant throughput of solders as they moved to Northern Ireland, Germany, Cyprus and the other operational bases of the army in the late 70s. Tracking them all down, interviewing them and corroborating their statements would have been impossible, so hard decisions had to be made and a highly selective approach taken, with only men who matched certain criteria being interviewed. We now know that it was a red herring and that the energy expended was wasted. It was, however, a task the original squad could not shirk and, scanning the now yellowed original forms, it was obvious they had done the job intelligently and well.

Much work was also done on the description of the clothes worn by the two men. One of them wore very distinctive high-waisted trousers with a row of buttons. This fashion feature was given extensive media exposure with artists' impressions carried by various newspapers and inquiries carried out as far away as London's Carnaby Street and other leading fashion areas. In a period of bizarre styles, the search came to nothing.

Then, of course, there were the local suspects – the sex offenders and rapists who lived and had offended in the area. One by one, they were traced, interviewed and eliminated. There were no hot contenders – the scenes of crime and forensics yielded nothing that we could use at the time. Gradually, amidst the thousands of leads, reality dawned – there were no real quality nuggets of information to pursue. Helen and Christine had disappeared from the pub that night and, six months later, a large squad of the ablest detectives of their day, supported by huge public backing and active media, were no further forward than they had been on the weekend that the bodies had been found.

I remember the palpable feeling of frustration and self-doubt within the CID at the time. How could a crime of such enormity happen here and, having happened, how could we fail to solve it?

As the lines of investigation each gradually reached a dead end, the inevitable decision was taken. The World's End murder inquiry, one of the most important crimes to be investigated by Lothian and Borders Police in modern times, was to be shelved until and unless a new substantial line of inquiry was established. It was a big decision to make in such a high-profile case but it was not the end. There was a clear sense of unfinished business and a strong belief that the answer would come. Looking back, I'm certain it was this mindset of unfinished business that ensured the inquiry was moth-balled in such an efficient way. In those days, before computerised systems, unsolved cases were boxed – literally put in a cardboard box or boxes – and stored in an old record room, where, over the years, they were frequently rifled for information or old statements. With officers constantly going back over the paperwork, witness statements and police records were seldom returned to their original state. The World's End was different – the original squad were convinced their work would be revisited so nothing was left to chance. All the files were completed, the indexes brought up to date and, in the old laboratory on the top floor of the Fettes HQ, Lester Knibb and his colleagues carefully stored all the forensic samples. Helen's recovered clothing, samples from the sites where the bodies were found, swabs from the post-mortems and, crucially, all the ligatures, with the knots still in place, were carefully sealed away awaiting the breakthrough all believed would one day come.

Over the years, bits and pieces of information came in – some-times it was the name or names of suspects arrested for a serious crime elsewhere and sometimes a piece of gossip or malice. And there was the usual flurry of information that would follow the times when the news was slow and local papers printed their regular 'great unsolved mysteries' articles.

By the 1980s, the responsibility for the World's End had been handed to the East and Midlothian Division for ongoing care and maintenance. As the division 'where the bodies lay' or had been found, this was the long-established procedure.

Reading through the old paper files, it struck me that the

successive officers who took responsibility for the World's End could have hardly been of a higher quality if they had been hand-picked. But I suppose in a sense they were. There was always a feeling that the World's End was special, sacred, and that it was being held in trust until the breakthrough came. The list of officers in charge included some of the most respected of their day: George Ritchie, eventually a head of CID, whose son Andy was destined to be a key player in the 2004 team; Kenny Shanks, a formidable detective, whose family have served Lothian and Borders Police for generations; Detective Inspector Stuart Anderson, who was involved throughout his service; and latterly Superintendent John McGowan, a fastidious, meticulous and tenacious man who did so much to highlight the case and champion its continued investigation; then finally Ian Thomas and the indefatigable Allan Jones, who was to see it through to the end.

Long service in the police can sour people – repeated exposure to the worst of human nature can make you cynical, negative and lose faith – but for some this never happens and they keep their early passion, their idealism and, above all, their belief. The World's End inquiry was served by such people over the years. Any doubts officers newly assigned to the case might have would be quickly dispelled when they read files, examined the photographs and gazed at the last pictures to be taken of Helen and Christine alive – two happy, healthy young girls, barely more than children. That was always enough to stir the spirit and motivate any police officer with pride in the job.

And it wasn't all about senior detectives – it never is. The senior detectives take the credit and the blame, their reputations are made or destroyed, but the truth is that it's the rank and file that do the job or not. So it was with the World's End. From top to bottom, through the generations, they never gave up and they just kept going. There were people like Athene Moir, a typist in the incident room off and on for most of the thirty-year investigation. She lived and breathed the inquiry. She was there at the start and, along with Lester Knibb, she was there at the end. She carried no police rank, she didn't make the headlines but no one was more dedicated to the task than she was.

It would be a long nine years after the case was mothballed before any substantial new information surfaced to give the investigation new impetus. During that time, the numerous leads that had found their way to the police were of insufficient quality to warrant a new squad and were dealt with by some of the experienced hands at Dalkeith CID, many of whom had served on the original inquiry.

In 1988, the force received what appeared to be the information they needed to make a major breakthrough in the dormant case. They were contacted by an inmate of Edinburgh's Saughton Prison who told them that a cellmate had confessed to him one night that he was responsible for the killings. What made this lead so important was that the man who contacted us had been able to give details of the case that had not been made public. Especially significant was his description of how the bodies had been left.

On the face of it, this was very promising so a new team was set up and investigations begun. Members of the girls' families were also alerted to the development. This burst of activity coincided with the first emergence of DNA technology as an investigatory tool. It was not the obvious first step it is today and significant inquiries had been made by the time the suspect was arrested and DNA swabs taken, but hopes were dashed by the scientists who were able to categorically say that the new suspect was not our man.

There were two other significant leads thrown up around the turn of the decade that are worth mentioning. One resulted from the decision to send officers to the doors of some of Edinburgh's better known criminals. During these inquiries, a man came forward sometime about 1992 to say that he had been joyriding in a stolen car in the Aberlady area on the night of the killings and he had picked up a man called John McGrannigan who was a convicted rapist. Quite why our informant had waited for fifteen years to pass this on was of course suspicious but circumstances and loyalties change and it looked as if we had a lead and a promising lead at that. Intelligence files revealed that we suspected that McGrannigan's brother Charlie had been murdered by a well-known city gangster to silence him. Quite what it was he was to be silenced for was not spelt out in the intelligence reports but officers concluded, not unreasonably, that it just might have been connected to the World's End case. However, once again, after a thorough investigation, John McGrannigan was also cleared by the fledging DNA technology and we were back to square one.

It may seem odd to some that we bother with any additional inquiries when DNA profiling is available. It's simple – to secure a conviction, we need best evidence, we need corroboration, we need more than DNA. While DNA profiling may have entered the public psyche as infallible, it is not regarded as such by the courts and is very often subjected to rigorous challenge by the defence. Often an approach to the suspect is the last phase of an investigation, done at a time when sufficient evidence has been gathered to justify the detention, questioning and even the arrest of the person concerned.

So this latest lead was concluded. Our informant, McGrannigan and the man thought complicit in his brother's death were all interviewed and each of them had their DNA tested. The test results eliminated them once and for all from the inquiry.

However, it was also in 1992 that another tantalising lead came along and, while it was treated less urgently, it remained on file for some time before it was eventually ruled out. A woman came forward to report that her ex-husband had abandoned her and left the country shortly after the killings. To enrich the story, she added that he had owned a pair of highly distinctive trousers similar to those worn by one of the men seen with Helen and Christine and which had been the subject of considerable publicity. The old adage about hell having no fury like a women scorned did occur to the detectives given the job of following up the lead. Nonetheless, no chances could be taken. An international search was begun and, some time later, the police in Germany ran the fugitive husband to ground. The inquiry team was unsurprised when his DNA was checked and he was cleared.

In 1997, a more complete DNA profile was isolated from Helen Scott's clothing. This prompted a new review of the entire case – a fresh look through fresh eyes with the benefit of new science. A famous murder squad detective from New York once said that 'sometimes the difference between failure and success is a new thought'. The new science was generating some new thinking in the World's End case.

By this time, the fastidious Superintendent John McGowan was in charge and he quickly established a base with a small hand-picked team at Dalkeith police station. The plan was simple and logical. They would progress the case through a structured and thorough review of all the old files and then, after drawing up a new list of suspects, they would begin to interview or reinterview those on the list and, where possible, obtain DNA samples to compare with the recently discovered samples from Helen's coat. Exactly twenty years after the murders, John McGowan and his team were ready to start again but, this time, they were not relying solely on interview and alibi – now they had an evidential ace up their sleeve. If they got a sample of the man's DNA, they could be absolutely sure he was or was not connected to the case.

I was an assistant chief constable working at Force Headquarters when this development was going on and the mood was optimistic – the whole force felt that this time we had a real chance to solve the case. If the culprits were in the system and if they were still alive, we would get to them eventually.

After a painstaking review of all the paperwork – literally

thousands of documents from the original case – the most promising lines of inquiry were prioritised and details of them were entered on to the new HOLMES computerised database. This back record conversion from paper-based to the computerised HOLMES system was laborious and time-consuming but it was essential to modernise the original inquiry.

The first phase of the investigation was to get DNA samples from the men we knew had been in the World's End after 10 p.m. on the night Helen and Christine disappeared. Then we would do the same with the dozens of named suspects who had been suggested over the intervening years and whose names remained on the files after they had not been fully eliminated. In addition to these priorities, about 1,200 individuals were also flagged on the Police National Computer. They were of lower priority but, if or when they were arrested anywhere in the UK, we asked that their DNA be obtained for elimination.

We seemed to be heading in the right direction but, despite our early hopes, this phase gave us no direct hits. None of our named suspects matched the DNA profile and no one we had traced from the World's End on the night of the murders came close either. Over 200 samples had been sent for costly DNA analysis but, despite the disappointing outcome, it had still been an important exercise – not least because some long-standing inquiries had now been cleared up and the names of some people who had not been fully eliminated in the original investigation had now been removed from the list of suspects.

The planned second phase, an extension of the DNA search, was postponed. In 1999 the Mid and East Lothian Division of Lothian and Borders was stretched to the limits by an unprecedented series of murders and serious crime, including a double assassination near Tranent, a former mining town east of Edinburgh. Some of the World's End officers had to be redeployed in order to meet the challenges the force faced. Then the latest champion of the World's

End, John McGowan, retired and the impetus was lost for the moment but such is the fate of historic or cold case inquiries. Urgent current demands take priority and this often means that old cases, no matter how important, have to be temporarily set aside.

The World's End was not set aside for long, however. A chance meeting between then Detective Sergeant Allan Jones and a visiting lecturer at the Scottish Police College at Tulliallan saw to that.

Allan, a Midlothian-trained detective, was steeped in the World's End inquiry even though the crime had been committed before he joined the police. He had played a part in the latest reinvestigation and he was convinced that the case was solvable. The lecturer visiting the Police College was Detective Sergeant Andy McKay from the newly formed National Crime and Operations Faculty (NCOF). They fell into conversation and the subject soon turned to the World's End murders. Allan's enthusiasm was infectious and Andy McKay soon offered a structured cold case review – a technique pioneered by NCOF.

The offer was quickly accepted. By this time, the man in charge at Dalkeith CID was Craig Dobbie. Then a detective chief inspector, he would later investigate the horrific murder of another very young woman, Jodi Jones. He saw the huge potential of NCOF and worked as quickly as he could to bring their best people north to carry out one of their first comprehensive reviews in Scotland. NCOF was as good as their word and, in January 2001, the World's End investigation was subjected to its third thorough examination.

It was clear from the start that the ever-advancing DNA technology was to be the key. All the important non-scientific work that could have been done had been done. The real potential now lay in the forensic samples and particularly the knots of the gags and bindings, all carefully preserved and undisturbed for over twenty years. Then there was the DNA profile we had already identified. We had to be sure that, as we progressed, this continued to be compared against all databases. It was also decided to widen the search and through Interpol ten countries that had significant databases were contacted. The unique profile of the World's End killer was now being searched for from the USA to New Zealand. If he was there, we were confident we would find him. Discussion of why we had only one DNA profile and yet we were of the firm belief that two men had been involved in the girls' rapes and murders will follow in the next chapter.

More locally, all the suspects already cleared were checked and double-checked in case any errors had been made. We all felt we were close, very close, but still we lacked the breakthrough we so desperately needed.

4

The Breakthrough

DNA is a reduced form of the biochemical term 'deoxyribonucleic acid'. It is a complex self-replicating material found in every single cell of the body and has been described as the building block of life. Like fingerprints, no two examples of DNA are identical. But DNA is more useful in solving crimes than fingerprints because, unlike fingerprints, it contains clues as to its ancestral source. That is why, for instance, the Duke of Edinburgh provided scientists with samples of his DNA when they were trying to identify bones found in a Russian burial pit a few miles north of Yekaterinburg. The bones were thought to be those of the imperial family murdered by the Bolsheviks in 1918. The Duke is not a direct descendant of the Romanovs but, through the complicated inter-breeding of the royal houses of Europe, he is related closely enough to them for a balance of probability calculation to be made. In the Russian case, that balance was sufficient to convince the Moscow authorities that the bones were those of Tsar Nicholas II and his family and, because of this, they were accorded a state funeral.

DNA profiling, also known as genetic fingerprinting, did not appear on the police radar until the late 1980s when the importance of the technique became apparent and detectives started turning to scientists for help in this new miracle aid to detection.

Lothian and Borders Police were at the forefront of forces seeking help in investigations. Like most forces, we had a number

54

of unsolved high-profile murder cases and officers were keen to explore any avenue that might lead to a resolution.

The first time DNA profiling was considered in the World's End case was in 1988 when the force was exploring a new lead that had been provided to us by a member of the public. That person had supplied specific information involving two identified potential suspects for the murders and the quality of the lead was such that a substantial inquiry was commenced.

Lester Knibb, the Lothian and Borders forensic scientist who had been at the crime scenes in 1977, took Helen Scott's coat to a company called Cellmark in Cambridge. At the time, Cellmark was blazing a trail in this fast-developing area of technology. The Cambridge scientists managed to isolate and then partially identify a DNA profile contained in semen staining on the garment. Cellmark were not able to give us complete genetic fingerprinting for the source of the staining but what they were able to tell us was enough to allow the two new suspects to be eliminated. Like all high-profile cases, the vast number of false leads was a feature of the World's End inquiry over the years and, being able to close this one down, through the benefit of this new technology, was a big advantage.

A fact seldom recognised is that the new science of DNA testing serves just as effectively to protect the innocent as it does to convict the guilty. In the last ten years, numerous 'good suspects' for serious crimes across the country have been quickly eliminated from suspicion by providing a DNA sample. One can only speculate but, in another time, without the assistance of this new science, the end result may have been different for some of those suspects.

Returning to the case, it was clear to senior officers as the 80s were turning into the 90s that DNA technology was advancing at a rapid rate. Its great problem, in those days, was that testing was a fairly destructive process that rendered the sample useless for further analysis. A decision was taken then not to subject the coat to more testing, as it would leave us without further samples if or when the technology improved to the extent that it might in the future be able to provide a complete profile of the suspect. This was a prudent decision for, in the early days of DNA profiling, many valuable forensic samples were tested to destruction with no result. Had they been preserved until more sensitive testing systems were developed things may have been different.

Next it was the turn of scientists employed by our neighbouring force Strathclyde Police. They had committed substantial resources to their forensic science service developing less destructive analytical process. They worked on the samples for some months before the painstaking examination by scientists Ian Hamilton and Martin Fairly paid off and they were able to identify a DNA match between the semen samples taken from Helen and Christine. That is to say Hamilton and Fairly were able to conclude that both girls had had sex with the same man.

As this work was going on in Glasgow, a database of DNA profiles was being established for the whole of the UK. Such was the quality of the latest results that officers overseeing the World's End case felt they had enough to go a stage further and have these DNA samples placed on this rapidly evolving database and compared for possible matches.

The procedures set up to protect the credibility of the database were such that only profiles achieved from a small number of accredited laboratories were able to be included. So it was that the Forensic Science Service in Wetherby had its initial involvement in the case. This was the move that allowed a full male DNA profile of the girls' attacker to be completed for the first time.

These breakthroughs were remarkable, of that there is no doubt. What was to follow in their wake was breathtaking.

By the first year of the new millennium, the science had evolved to the state that it was felt worthwhile to begin to examine other articles and samples gathered from the 1977 crime scene to see what secrets they held.

The Breakthrough

In 1977 the care taken of productions was of a lower standard than it is today. Nowadays, as scenes of crime are investigated, the possible presence of what is known as low-copy number DNA is very much to the front the officers' minds. If DNA was a major breakthrough, the discovery of low-copy DNA is, to employ a rather overused phrase these days, quite awesome. The essence of low-copy DNA technology is that microscopic particles of skin, hair or body fluids may not yield a full profile or be enough for an exact match but they could be sufficient to eliminate large sections of the community or point to the probability of a familial link with profiles on the database. In other words, it is not the cast-iron certainty of a full match but is rather a pointer, a lead to take investigators and scientists in a particular direction. Low-copy DNA has its risks – in particular, there is the possibility of cross-contamination – but, in the hands of the skilled investigator, its potential is enormous.

The discovery of only one DNA profile in the case had long baffled officers. Initially science suggested one man abducted, assaulted and murdered the two girls. That seemed unlikely because of the difficulty one man would have controlling two young women. On the other hand, sex offenders tend to work alone. It was with this in mind that Lester Knibb and his scientist colleague Derek Scrimger began considering if the new technology involving low-copy DNA would be able to help us. It was possible only one man was involved in the sexual assault part of these crimes but that a second man may have been an accessory and left his mark elsewhere in the crime scene.

Careful thought was given to where low-copy DNA may have survived the initial examination by detectives in 1977 and the passage of time. The conclusion of the scientists was that there was a time capsule within the forensic materials – a place that had been left undisturbed and unexamined since the time when the crimes were committed. That place was the centre of the knots used to bind the girls. The secrets locked in these bindings had the

57

potential to produce vital clues to the identities of Helen and Christine's killers. Such was the advance in forensic science that, if you had suggested a breakthrough like this was possible to the detectives of the 70s, the response would have been bewilderment and disbelief. However, that was exactly where the next stage of this scientific mystery tour was to take us to and with considerable success.

This part of the story is a great example of how the determination of officers involved in the World's End case has paid off over the years. By this time, the responsibility of the inquiry rested with Detective Superintendent Ian Thomas and the then Detective Inspector Allan Jones. They were typical of a long line of able and dedicated detectives who, over the years, worked with the scientists to keep the World's End case alive. Ian and Allan had come through the same route to hold senior ranks in the CID. They were both career detectives with long experience across a wide range of investigations. Ian's experience was mainly in the City while Allan's service had predominantly been in the County. They are very different individuals but they shared invaluable traits essential to successful detectives, they were imaginative, energetic and stubborn – they never, but never, gave up. When an obstacle blocked their path, they worked until they found a way round it and the potential obstacle was sometimes me.

As the investigation ground on, the costs rose and there were always other priorities. Time without number over the years, Ian, Allan or their predecessors would come to me to plead their case for funding. Money was tight but they always convinced me as to the merits of their case. Their passion and commitment made them impossible to deny. It was just as well for I am convinced that, without them and those who went before them, the World's End case would have remained a mystery to this day.

Ian and Allan had long realised that new developments in forensic science held the key and they had regular formal and informal meetings with colleagues like scientists Lester Knibb and Derek Scrimger and people from further afield, ever hopeful of hearing of a new technique, a development that could help this case.

So it must have been with a sense of excitement and anticipation that Allan Jones turned up at Wetherby in the spring of 2002 with the carefully preserved tights and belt that had been used to bind the girls. This was only to be partially fruitful. The Forensic Science Service were able to say yes there was recoverable and identifiable DNA at the centre of the knots but there was insufficient to allow any meaningful progress to be made on the already established but unidentified sample from the semen.

The findings from Wetherby did, however, produce sufficient information for officers to embark on a major new line of inquiry unparalleled since the early days of the case. The total absence of a match on the DNA database led my force to go off on what could only be described as an elimination exercise. The profile we had was of sufficiently high quality that the scientists were certain that, if we were able to find a relative of the source of the sample, we would be able to home in on the culprit. So it was that officers embarked on one of the biggest operations in the case since the original inquiry – a venture known as a Familial Search Operation. Swabs were issued to hundreds of men and they were asked to use them to provide us with a sample of their DNA. All the swabs were analysed and, if everything went to plan, there was a good chance that the extended family of the culprit would be discovered.

There were sufficient reference points in the DNA chain of the partially profiled sample that we had for it to be compared to DNA profiles on the national database and near matches extracted. We could then speak to those who were near matches and check their criminal records and those of their families to see if that would lead us to a perfect match. There is little need for me to say here just what an expensive, labour-intensive and painstaking process this kind of work is and, inevitably, for the teams involved in such tasks, morale is at first high but it begins to flag as time passes without any positive results.

Having drawn a blank in the east of Scotland, it was decided to try the same operation in the west which, due to the fact that the population is many times greater, would be an even bigger and more difficult job.

It was at this point that the breakthrough which had eluded us for twenty-six years came about. As so often happens in these cases, it was one we were not expecting.

In the trawling operation centred on Edinburgh, we had been looking for a general match of nuclear DNA, often abbreviated to nDNA. This is the type of DNA that is most helpful to forensic scientists as it contains more useful genetic information than its counterpart, mitochondrial DNA – that is to say it offers a wide range of variables that can be examined.

During the month of January 2004, great effort and thought were put into trying to come up with a different approach to what was a massive task and one that had no certainty of success. We were advised it would be sensible to isolate the Y chromosome of our DNA sample and use that alone as the control for the testing in the west of Scotland. The point of this approach was twofold. Firstly, unlike other elements of DNA, Y chromosomes do not change from father to son and, secondly, being able to concentrate on checking just one part of the profile would be faster and more cost efficient so it would allow us to put more resources into following up potential matches.

So it was that Allan Jones and his colleagues set off for yet another DNA testing laboratory with specialist techniques, this time in Birmingham, to isolate the Y chromosome in the coat sample and begin what would inevitably turn into an operation stretching out over many months. Fate intervened and two forensic scientists in Birmingham were able to give us the evidence we needed to put a name to the man we had been searching for all these years, but amazingly it wasn't the man who had left the original marks. While they were working on the coat sample to isolate the Y chromosome of the first sample, they discovered what we had suspected all along – there was not just one DNA code there but two. All the time, a second identifiable sample of DNA, in a much smaller quantity, had been there, masked by the more prevalent profile. It was confirmation of what we had believed all along – two men had been involved in the murders of Helen and Christine – and now, for the first time, we had the complete DNA profile of both of them.

One weekend in early spring 2004, I got a phone call from Roger Orr, our head of CID, saying that Ian and Allan urgently wanted to meet me. The importance of the breakthrough can be gauged by the fact that we didn't wait until the Monday to discuss it. Instead, on the Sunday afternoon, we met in my office at Fettes Headquarters. When I was told of the development, Ian and Allan's elation was clear for all to see. This is exactly what they had hoped would happen – because of their ability to shine a light back through time, the scientists had picked out the killers who had evaded normal policing techniques for so long. All their efforts had not been in vain.

Their elation was even more justified when it emerged that the new profile, the one belonging to the long-concealed second man, had matched one that was already on the national register of DNA profiles. We'd got a hit – it meant there would be no familial chain to work along, no difficult cross-referencing to be done and no statistical analyses to be carried out. The profile found in Birmingham was that of Angus Robertson Sinclair.

The name was vaguely familiar to some of us as he had, we recalled, fairly recently stood trial for a sex killing in Glasgow. The Scottish Criminal Records Office told us that Sinclair already had a prolific history of abduction and violent sex crime. At long last, we had one of the men involved in the World's End case firmly in the frame. One way or another, we were certain he would lead us to the second.

The low-copy DNA testing of the knots on the items used to bind the girls also indicated the presence of Sinclair. And elements of three other low-copy DNA samples were found – that of each of the girls themselves plus another which matched the dominant DNA profile obtained from the coat. This reinforced the theory that two men had been involved throughout.

So it was that Operation Trinity came into being. Now we had a suspect, it was time to see if there was concrete evidence of his involvement in any of the other unsolved killings in Scotland that, over the years, had been linked to the World's End case.

Testing of samples recovered from Helen's body also revealed Sinclair's DNA in much smaller quantities which is why it too had been masked for all these years by the dominant sample. In the case of Christine Eadie, it was more difficult. She had been left naked and her outer clothing was never found. However, the bra used to gag her had traces of DNA which could have belonged to Sinclair and strings of what could have been Sinclair's DNA were also found amongst the unidentified male DNA profile in samples taken from Christine's body.

All in all, the scientists were building up a pretty comprehensive picture of the likely sequence of events all those years ago on that dreadful night in Edinburgh and East Lothian. We now had a number-one suspect who we had discovered already had convictions that would put him right in the offender profile for a likely perpetrator of the World's End murders. We also had the original DNA profile that we hadn't been able to match on the database so now the challenge was to try to put a name to it. We believed this could be done by careful investigation of our named suspect's life around the time of the killings. If we could find out who he associated with, who his friends were, who he might have been with in Edinburgh that night in October 1977, we might be on to something. The next step would be to take this hopefully small group of people, gather DNA samples from each, conduct the analysis and, with any luck, we would find the answer.

But tangential to the high-tech scientific approach to the case, there would have to be an old-fashioned police inquiry involving officers interviewing and reinterviewing witnesses from the first inquiry and then building up a massively detailed background knowledge of our suspect. This sort of in-depth investigation is tough enough at the best of times but, given the number of intervening years, it would be taxing indeed. When viewed from 2004, the fact that Bing Crosby had died the day before Christine and Helen were murdered was not the great aid to the memory it had once been.

We would be revisiting evidence that, when it was originally found, may not have been viewed as significant but, now that we knew the identity of one of the killers, had the potential to become rather important. We also were aware of the fact that it was entirely likely that we would uncover other crimes committed by this individual. Quite what those would be was of course, at that stage, just another mystery but, in the fullness of time, details of any other crimes committed by the suspect could help us build a better picture and so it was to be.

The first part of our task was to build up as complete a profile as possible of the man the DNA told us was our prime suspect, a painter and decorator, now a prisoner in his fifties by the name of Angus Robertson Sinclair. This man had already shocked the country with his depraved offending but his name would soon for ever be linked with the World's End killings.

5

Angus Sinclair

The DNA identification of one of the men at the scene of the World's End killings was the breakthrough in the investigation we had waited a generation for. It had seemed clear on that first Sunday afternoon thirty years ago when the girls' bodies were found that we were almost certainly looking for two men – and they were men of the utmost brutality. It seemed equally certain that anyone capable of such callous acts was unlikely to be a first offender. The abduction and murder of two young women can be no accident. Such coolness of execution is not likely to have been the culmination of events that had started off with innocent intentions and had perhaps somehow got out of hand. It seemed to us that the crime was the premeditated conclusion of a carefully planned operation or at least the likely outcome.

The eventual isolation of one person's DNA and the match on the police database to Angus Robertson Sinclair took us on a journey through the depths of criminality to a man who allowed nothing to stand in the way of his violent sexual urges and thereafter not only showed no remorse for what he had done but actually demonstrated over time utter contempt for his victims.

In his book *The Amber Spyglass*, Philip Pullman writes: 'Good and evil are names for what people do, not what they are.' In my experience, this is usually true in that most murders are not premeditated; they are usually the tragic consequence of a moment's madness or passion – a loss of control that ends a life and changes the lives of many others for ever.

Many murderers have no other convictions, are not career criminals and, like their victims, are sometimes simply in the wrong place at the wrong time in the wrong state of mind. I have sat with a good number of murderers immediately after their arrest. For the most part, they are frightened, nervous, pathetic individuals – more often to be pitied than despised. It's a popular misconception that policemen feel anger, rage and righteous indignation when arresting people for murder – some may but the usual feeling is one of sadness and regret for the tragic waste of life. As far as that large percentage of murderers is concerned, Pullman is undoubtedly right but there are also those who must fall into another category. These include the sadists, the psychopaths, the sociopaths, the multiple killers and, probably worst of all, the child killers – people like the Moors murderers, Ian Brady and Myra Hindley; Robert Black who killed little Susan Maxwell, Caroline Hogg and Sarah Harper; and, more recently, the Soham killer, Ian Huntley. In terms of the planning, the repetition, the cruel indifference to suffering and the cool demeanour they show in the aftermath of their crimes, these individuals challenge Pullman's theory. I believe there are evil people – evil people whose actions put them beyond any forgiveness or sympathy – and Angus Robertson Sinclair is one of them.

The catalogue of crime Sinclair had been convicted of by the time our investigation into his background began was already one of the worst in Scottish criminal history. It was a criminal record sufficient to earn him a place in the premier league of notorious offenders across the UK. Since 1982, Sinclair has been in jail continuously and is unlikely ever to be released. For some reason, however, Sinclair was not widely known to the public and had managed to escape the notoriety his crimes deserved to have marked him with. Whilst they have all been extensively reported, such is the time span of his offending and the gaps between his arrests that the totality of it seems to have slipped by. It is almost as though the constituent parts of his criminal record have not been added up so that the full range of his crimes has not been apparent – until now.

He has, in fact, been known to the police for most of his life but, because of his cunning, his fastidious attention to detail and some degree of luck, together with the careful way in which victims were selected, I am convinced that he has escaped the kind of intense police scrutiny he deserved. He got away with too much for too long.

Let me say at this point that I firmly believe it is entirely likely that locked away in the mind of this man are details of many more horrific crimes that we will never know of. We certainly uncovered irrefutable evidence of serious violent offending, robberies and non-sexual assaults as part of our inquiry into his past – crimes that all bore the Sinclair hallmark in that they were chilling in their violence and displayed callous disregard for people's lives and suffering. Who knows what else lies hidden by the passage of time?

Being a criminal is not like a normal career with recognisable routes to the top of your chosen trade or profession. Most crimes, especially violent ones, are unplanned and haphazard. The most successful criminals are never caught. It often amuses police officers to see notorious underworld figures described as top criminals when, in fact, they have spent half their lives in jail. The truth is that their notoriety, by definition, makes them failures. Being caught and having a long criminal record are hardly an indication of success – remember that the next time you see Mad Findlay or Crazy Charlie on a television chat show. If they were that good, how come they got caught and convicted so often? It is the ones that are never caught, the ones you never hear of who are the true professionals.

Amongst sexual offenders, however, there is often a clear pattern of escalating seriousness of offence as the perpetrator becomes increasingly more confident in his ability to avoid detection or as the need for ever greater thrills drives him deeper into depravity. That is not to say that all minor offenders go on to carry out more serious offences. They don't but the thefts of knickers from washing lines can lead to more serious crimes and they cannot be ignored. Left unchecked, the park flasher can sometimes go on to become the park rapist if their behaviour is not confronted. Most sex offenders arrested for serious crimes have clues in their backgrounds, pointers to what their future behaviour might be. Some have minor sex crime convictions and many have been victims themselves. One of the greatest challenges of managing lesser sex offenders is the difficulty in spotting the ones who are likely to continue to offend and, worse, those whose offences will escalate and become ever more serious. Social workers and the police are often criticised when it goes wrong. With hindsight, it's always easy to spot the ones who are going to become serious offenders – the tabloids are very good at it – but, in the real world, it is very hard. Looking at a range of people with similar convictions, it's almost impossible to sit down and do an analysis of the circumstances and predict which men will cease offending, which will stay at the same level and which will become a major danger to society.

Brought up in some of the toughest areas of Glasgow, Sinclair did not follow any established pattern. His first crimes were of a relatively minor nature and involved theft and housebreaking, albeit at a very young age – he was fourteen at his first court appearance. But, in the Glasgow of the late 50s when he would have been in his mid teens, these offences would not have been out of the ordinary amongst his peers. It would, however, not be long before the juvenile offender Sinclair would be back in court – as a teenage killer.

As I begin to describe the background of Sinclair and his criminal history, it will quickly become clear just what a very dangerous person he has always been. As I have already said, he shows a contempt towards his victims that is breathtaking. Worse than that, in a criminal career of serious offending stretching back almost forty-five years, he has never once, to the knowledge of officers who have carried out meticulous inquiries into his life, expressed the slightest remorse. This is not just my view and those of other police officers but the firm conclusion of every professional to have come across him in the criminal justice system since he was twelve years old. Eventually at the conclusion of our inquiries when he was confronted with his past he would have the chance to show remorse for what he had done but, during countless hours of detailed interviews with skilled officers who were thoroughly prepared for their task, there was not a glimmer of contrition. He had nothing to lose – he was serving two life sentences, he was fifty-nine years of age, he knew he was never going to be released – yet he never once showed a sign of cracking. Rather there was a stony-faced and steady resolve to play the game to the end and, in the finest tradition of the career criminal, admit absolutely nothing.

Sinclair was the youngest of three children born to a couple who lived in the Maryhill area of Glasgow. Mary and Angus Sinclair had a fourteen-year-old son and an eleven-year-old daughter by the time Angus Junior came along. When his third child was born, Angus Senior was suffering from increasingly severe bouts of an illness which was eventually diagnosed as leukaemia. He spent a lot of time at the family home in St Peter's Street not far from the city centre. Although he was too ill to work, he was able to look after young Angus whilst mother Mary worked in a nearby tobacconist shop. Angus Senior died just four years after his youngest child was born and Mary Sinclair said she was naturally worried about how he would react to his dad's death. To begin with, his life progressed normally and he went first to nursery and then to the local primary school in nearby Grove Street.

In the background of many sex offenders, there is often a history of them having being victims of sexual abuse before going on to be perpetrators. On the face of it, it's counter-intuitive. You would think that, having been the victim of sex crime and being aware of the long-term solitary suffering that goes with it, the last thing someone would want to do is to carry it on and repeat the victimisation. Yet time and time again we find this is exactly what happens with victims becoming offenders and on and on, creating a pyramid of suffering. This was not the case with Sinclair. Although he alleged it, we found no evidence at all to suggest that he had been a victim. He had a tough upbringing but no tougher than thousands of others.

The Glasgow of his childhood was the Glasgow of *No Mean City* fame. It was also a time of upheaval in Scotland's largest city as great social changes were taking place. Huge areas of the inner city were designated as slums and bulldozed with the residents decanted to estates on the outskirts as well as the new towns that were springing up across the Central Belt of Scotland. This was the Glasgow of gangs and violence where murder rates ran far ahead of the rest of the country and local crime lords sorted out their differences with knives and razors and then, increasingly, guns. It was during Sinclair's teenage years that a period of peace was brought to parts of Glasgow by the unlikely figure of the singer Frankie Vaughan. He became involved with youth work in the east end of the city and ultimately brokered a deal between rival gangs and persuaded them to join in a weapons amnesty. Sinclair may not have been directly involved in this but it is important to describe this background to give an impression of the parts of the city in which he grew up. Glasgow was then a place where in some areas extreme violence was the currency of everyday life.

The eventual criminal trial would require us to have an exceptionally detailed knowledge of all aspects of Sinclair's life. A simple recitation of his criminal record and any surviving probation reports would not even begin to fill the need we had. We had to find ways to bridge the time gap, to stretch back more than forty years and gather together comprehensive details of his life, friends and movements – every scrap of information that could be gleaned to give us clues to his behaviour. As we set off on this task, our investigation was in its early days and it was impossible to gauge the totality of exactly the sort of information we were looking for, but officers knew that any single seemingly unimportant snippet may take on immense significance as the inquiry progressed. This was especially relevant in our search to trace the second man – the elusive source of our original DNA sample.

The first areas to explore were of course his friends and family. There were also the weighty reports drawn up by professionals involved in his various court appearances. Most people connected to Sinclair over the years were well disposed towards us and prepared to do all they could to help clear up these very serious crimes. Lengthy statements were taken from surviving members of his immediate family. As we have already noted, his father died when he was just a young boy and, by this time, his mother was long dead too.

One striking feature of his childhood was the close relationship the young Sinclair formed with his sister's daughter who, for her own protection, I will not name. It seems clear, as is often the case in these circumstances, that he had been led to believe that this girl was in fact his sister. Family members remember him being very affectionate towards her and when he was older using his pocket money to buy her quite generous gifts. His sister saw nothing untoward in this relationship. She recalled that at that time he seemed to be a happy and normal little boy. He would appear to have been generally well behaved in class at St George's Road Junior Secondary School where he completed his formal education. There was certainly nothing to worry about in his school reports. Despite the fact that he'd been in trouble with the police from a young age, they recorded him being of average intelligence and well mannered.

It was also apparent from the recall of family members that Sinclair spent a period of time in some sort of residential care though no one can remember the details of why this should have happened and no official records could be found. It may have been connected to the moody and depressive behaviour witnessed by family and teachers after his father's death. In those days, children were put into care for a variety of reasons which, unlike today, did not need to be explained or fully recorded. The stock phrase 'beyond parental control' covered a multitude of sins and often glossed over deep psychological problems. Perhaps the first clue to his future behaviour lay in that decision to take Angus into care – we will never know. What we do know is that his mother was becoming increasingly concerned.

Sinclair's criminal career started in earnest in 1959, when he was fourteen. His string of petty offences – theft, housebreaking, breaches of probation – are all gateway crimes you could see on a thousand young boys' records as they make the difficult transition through puberty in a bad neighbourhood and with the wrong crowd but it's the kind of bad start that many boys survive. The vast majority recover from starting out on the wrong foot – they grow out of their criminal ways and go on to be decent, sometimes even prominent, citizens. As they mature and have their ways mended – usually by a girlfriend or wife – their names disappear from the criminal records, often before they reach the age of twenty.

Because of this perennial trend, the Scottish criminal justice system does all it can not to stigmatise young offenders. The Children's Hearing System is criticised by many and it does have difficulty dealing with the small group of very active offenders but overall, for the 90 per cent who do not reoffend, it is absolutely the correct response. There are of course exceptions – those who start in their teens and don't stop, those who go on to be career criminals and leave in their wake dozens, even hundreds, of victims. Angus Sinclair was just such a man and it was at this very early age that the crimes of dishonesty which were a constant in his background were overtaken by the sex crimes that were to dominate his life and ensure his infamy.

In 1961 Sinclair appeared at Glasgow Sheriff Court charged with the offence under Scots law of lewd and libidinous behaviour. This is one of the minor charges available for sex offences and it is usually applied when inappropriate behaviour that falls short of sexual assault has taken place. In what was to be a first sign of his character and nature, he denied the offence which involved an eight-year-old girl who lived just a few doors from Sinclair's family home in St Peter's Street. Despite his protestations, he was convicted again and his future hung in the balance.

The social consequences were also dramatic. His actions were the talk of the neighbourhood and he lost his job, his first on leaving school at fifteen.

While awaiting sentence, Sinclair spent a period in a remand home where the authorities began having their first detailed look at his character without, it seems, any great success. He was again given probation – this time for three years. The probation officers who supervised him found him an enigma. He played the game, worked with the system he knew he could not beat and he never, never admitted his guilt. It is not all that unusual for a pubescent boy to be obsessed with sex but few carry out their fixation to the extremes that Sinclair was to – especially at fifteen years of age.

That fixation with sex turned to utter tragedy just six months later, in July 1961, when he was arrested for the murder of a seven-year-old girl who lived in the same tenement block as his first child victim in St Peter's Street. Not only was this killing carried out in the same place as the previous attack but it happened while he was still subject to the probation order for the first offence.

Reading contemporary reports of that case in my office in Livingston New Town over forty years later was a chilling experience. For someone so young to be capable of such a crime and then to deny it and calmly try to cover it up as he did showed that he was cool headed and detached beyond his years. With the benefit of hindsight I had that day, it was clear the killing of Catherine Reehill was an ominous sign of what was to come.

The newspapers of the day described what happened. Sinclair, still only fifteen, had been left alone in his home, a tenement flat in St Peter's Street. He would have been secure in the knowledge that none of his family would be returning for at least three hours. It was a narrow window of opportunity but it was enough and it seems to me that what followed was the execution of a carefully thought-through plan that was carried out with the cold single-mindedness, determination and the disregard for his victim that was to become Sinclair's signature in later crimes. The details of this crime were a first illustration of the modus operandi that would be used in later life. The events leading up to the death of the little girl on 1 July 1961 would be mirrored in crimes many years later. There was a carefully laid plan – gain the trust of the victim and then attack with overwhelming violence. Bear in mind that Maryhill in Glasgow in the 1960s was a close-knit and traditional community of working-class families who tended to spend their lives in and around the same areas. The families who lived in the tenements of St Peter's Street would have been there for years and would have been on first-name terms with every one of their immediate neighbours and on nodding terms with just about everyone in the neighbourhood.

Minutes after being left alone, Sinclair went out of the house, approached seven-year-old Catherine Reehill and asked her to run an errand for him. He sent her to the corner shop to buy him some chocolate and instructed her to bring it to his flat. A willing little helper, she quickly ran there and back, only to have Sinclair force himself on her. He tried to have sex with her but she fought him off, banging her head so badly in the struggle that there was blood everywhere. The details of what happened next do not need to be repeated in graphic terms here – suffice to say that he strangled the little girl and raped her.

One of the most telling features of this attack was that, as Sinclair was carrying out his deadly attack, he was interrupted. There was a knock on the door of the flat and Sinclair, in the middle of his murderous assault, opened the front door wide. He appeared totally calm to his caller, a friend and neighbour of similar age, and, after agreeing to meet later that night, Sinclair closed the door and returned to killing. That kind of detachment is very telling. To be caught in the act of murder and be able to divorce yourself so coolly from what is going on as to appear completely normal is hard to do. One could hardly expect that of a hardened criminal let alone a boy of fifteen. This was no crime of passion, committed through a loss of reason – it was a cold-hearted plan, carried through with precision.

In his eventual explanation of the crime, Sinclair said that, when he realised Catherine was dead, he carried her body out of the flat and down the common stair. He left it dumped at the bottom of the stairwell. There was of course no evidence to prove his version that she died from an 'accidental' blow to the head during the struggle. She may equally well have been bludgeoned by Sinclair. Knowing his character, it is unlikely that Sinclair would have wanted his victim to survive to tell what had happened to her. He always tried very hard to escape blame.

The child's crumpled corpse was found a short time later by a neighbour returning home and the alarm was raised. The position she had been left in made it appear as if the little girl had fallen down the steep stone stairs. Sinclair was one of the first on the scene and witnesses told how he was heard loudly demanding to know what had happened. The people who rushed to the stair brought by the neighbour's screams could not have been expected to guess at the truth of what had actually happened. At first they just presumed little Catherine had fallen downstairs. Sinclair alone at that point knew how wrong the neighbours' guesses actually were.

It was not long though before suspicion fell on him – perhaps because of his very recent past offences. He was detained by police and questioned several times during the following day. He denied all knowledge of what had happened to the little girl but detectives concluded that he was lying and he was charged with murder. Later that night, after speaking to his brother, who he had always respected, Sinclair made an admission of sorts. He told officers what had happened and why. He said he had lost control of his sexual urges, there had been a struggle and Catherine had banged her head.

Here was the first step up the ladder of offending and a steep one at that. He had, just months before, committed a sexually motivated offence against a young girl. In this latest crime, the offence was grave and the outcome tragic. Looking back all those years, one question stands out – had he already learned that leaving his victim alive would be a mistake? His explanation that Catherine had banged her head appears improbable – there seems to have been a clearly premeditated killing followed by an equally clear attempt to avoid its consequences yet retain some control by his presence at the scene. In the immediate aftermath of the discovery of Catherine's body, Sinclair visited his brother and attempted to establish an alibi. Looking back, it was clear to see that officers in July 1961 were dealing with quite a sophisticated pattern of offending from a very young man.

Whilst on remand, Sinclair would have been examined at length by psychiatrists. The reports that survived the years remain confidential – suffice to say that he remained detached and seemed not to accept the gravity of his deeds.

As we digested the reports into Sinclair piling up in the incident room and spoke to people who had had dealings with him over the years, it looked as though we were going to have a tough job getting through to him as we eventually hoped to do.

From the very first days after he was identified by the DNA profile from the evidence from the World's End crime scene, it was clear that, despite the passage of time and the fact that he was now in jail, Sinclair was not going to be an easy nut to crack.

Much of this early work had been carried out in secret but my experience of dealing with the press over the years left me convinced that we were not going to be able to maintain that secrecy for much longer. By that time 'Operation Trinity' was up and running, a large squad of officers was being assembled and I had been appointed Officer in Overall Command. As the inquiries grew more extensive and diverse, more officers from across Scotland became involved and a leak, either deliberate or accidental, would almost certainly occur. Inevitably we would have to go public on the investigation. It might be no bad thing for there was also the chance that some new information could come our way from the public following the widespread news coverage the inquiry would generate.

The downside would be that Sinclair would know what was happening and that, sooner or later, we would be knocking on his door. It would give him time to prepare himself – toughen himself mentally against what he knew was coming. It was our total determination that, when that day came, the officers interviewing him would know Sinclair as well as they knew their own families. They would know every aspect of his upbringing and offending. They would have a clear idea of his state of mind through detailed and painstaking study of all the various reports compiled over the years. They would also have a good idea of what he was like now. But what would the general demeanour of the man they would even-tually confront be like?

By the time Operation Trinity was up and running, Sinclair had been held in the unit for the detention and treatment of sex offenders at Peterhead Prison on Scotland's north-east coast for some years. The wing of the bleak-looking granite building dedi-cated to this work is universally known as the 'Beastie Block'. Because of this, most ordinary inmates find Peterhead objectionable and they also dislike its remote location because visitors from the Central Belt of Scotland have to spend many hours by car or public transport to get there. It isn't easy for somebody from Glasgow to visit a Peterhead inmate using public transport. The train journey takes at least two and a half hours and then there's a further hour on the bus from Aberdeen – although it does drop people off right outside the gates of the prison. Eight hours of travel from Glasgow and back and a two-hour visit makes for a long day.

Strangely, however, our initial soundings of staff at Peterhead suggested that Sinclair rather liked it there. In fact, it seemed he was something of a model prisoner. One official at the jail, no doubt with tongue in cheek, went as far as to say Sinclair was 'as reliable as some of the staff'.

It seems that quite early on in his stay at the jail he was given trusted inmate status and allowed to work in the kitchen. Within a relatively short space of time, he had earned the respect of the jail authorities and had more or less taken charge of the kitchen where he maintained a strict regime amongst his fellow inmate workers. He was given responsibility for ordering food and other supplies and in this he showed his characteristic organisational skills and appetite for hard work.

It is well known that sex offenders can often be subjected to a hard time in jail from other inmates. One of the virtues of the Peterhead unit from the inmates' point of view is that all prisoners have similar offending backgrounds and, as such, there is a much reduced chance of the kind of abuse or physical attacks they might face in a mainstream jail.

Sinclair, by all accounts, had adapted well to jail life. He was so confident of his own position in the jail pecking order that he was known to hand out ferocious reprimands to trusty workers in 'his' kitchen if they failed to match his exacting standards.

The picture we were getting of the 2004 Angus Robertson Sinclair was very different from the one that had inevitably been formed from even a casual reading of his criminal record. The older Sinclair took pride in his work and was, in many ways, a model inmate. It was as though he had somehow managed in his own mind to divorce himself from the reality of his background. The merciless sexual predator, who, throughout a long offending career, had shown not one jot of remorse for his action or pity to his victims, appeared to have changed. He was now so trusted by the authorities in the jail and by his fellow inmates that he had a special place in the hierarchy. Inmates sought his advice and counsel and the judgements he made of their circumstances were characterised as firm but fair.

It was against this background that, in consultation with the senior investigating officers of the forces involved investigating all the murders that came under the umbrella of Operation Trinity, we decided to go public with details of our operation. I hoped to stop unhelpful publicity that might result from a leak from a source not fully in the picture of what we were doing and even perhaps bring forward new witnesses to any of the individual cases.

I had no intention of revealing the name of our prime suspect nor even confirming it to reporters but I was aware that some of the news outlets with well-connected crime reporters knew exactly who our suspect was. At a press conference at police headquarters in Edinburgh, I sat down, flanked by senior officers from the other forces involved, to give an overview of the operation minus many of the details the press wanted and we needed to protect at this stage. We said we were interested in the unsolved murders of seven young women. At the time of this conference, we were still considering the possible connection of Sinclair to two unsolved murders in Dundee although, when I sat down that day, there were increasing doubts that these killings were connected to our inquiries. Already the few potential links with the Dundee murders were beginning to look a little shaky but the inclusion of those cases in Trinity gave them new impetus and brought forward new lines of inquiry.

The following morning's papers were full of the story, naming Sinclair and giving extensive details on his background. Many experienced journalists in Scotland knew of the cases we were dealing with and there had been previous speculation concerning Sinclair in some quarters. As the case was not at this stage active, which is to say *sub judice* and protected by the Lord Advocate's Guidelines and the Contempt of Court Act, the press could say virtually what they wanted without fear of the consequences. Few, if any, mentioned that first killing, that of Catherine Reehill, and we were pleased to see some other sensitive areas of the investigations had escaped the attention of reporters.

As our background inquiries into Sinclair progressed, we un-covered a lot of the detailed information about that first fatal sex attack. Aspects of it were highly unusual and we would find them repeated in later crimes. He had spoken of his sexual activity prior to the killing of little Catherine. Most of it had been conducted in association with other boys. He and one particular friend had been in the habit of having sex with either of two girls who had made themselves available in return for cigarettes. Usually though it was Sinclair and his friend having sex with the same girl on the same night. He seemed to like to have a chum at hand. There was also a suggestion from Sinclair that one of his friends had warned him of the dangers of sexually transmitted diseases. This obviously struck home for later he certainly seemed to have had a severe phobia about it – though not severe enough to prevent him continuing his behaviour.

In the Reehill case, the Crown Office, the prosecuting authority, had decided they would not be able to prove premeditation in the killing of little Catherine and so Sinclair was charged with culpable homicide, the Scots law equivalent of manslaughter, and he pled guilty. Before sentence was passed in August 1961, the judge heard extracts of various reports, one passage of which is chilling in its accuracy as it predicted that no psychotherapy treatment would benefit such a sexual obsession and that young Sinclair would require constant supervision – failure to do this would result in continued sexual offending should he be given the slightest opportunity. These thoughts were prophetic indeed and, as we read them, they echoed down the years.

The judge, Lord Mackintosh, branded the teenager 'callous, cunning and wicked' and ordered that he be detained for ten years.

Reading the stark warnings contained in reports of over forty years ago and knowing what happened during the intervening period were sobering in the extreme. We could never say we had not been warned.

Despite being still only sixteen years old it was clear that, at the time, the authorities had no appropriate place to keep him and he was eventually held in the adult jail in Aberdeen for the first three years of his sentence. Who knows what lessons the young Sinclair was taught by older inmates and how this experience influenced his future behaviour? His time there may have even been the final building block in the creation of Sinclair and the public menace he was to become. During his stay in Aberdeen, he worked at joinery and net-making and had a spell in the cookhouse. Those monitoring his progress noticed how he formed firm friendships with older men, recidivists, and displayed a 'thinly veiled disregard for authority or guidance' – a dangerous omen of what was to come. Again, with hindsight, it seems wholly inappropriate that he was sent to an adult prison – young people of the age Sinclair was then should obviously not be in jail with adult prisoners. These days they would not be in an adult jail except in the most exceptional of circumstances and, if they were, the authorities would ensure they were closely monitored and held for as short a time as possible.

Sinclair stayed in Aberdeen until the mid 60s when he was transferred to Edinburgh with a view to his eventual release. One constant throughout this period of incarceration was a series of regular visits from his mother, Mary, and sister. It seems that they had rather fallen out with Sinclair's brother, who had obviously helped the detectives investigating Catherine Reehill's killing.

Sinclair's mother and sister made the long trip to Aberdeen at least once a month to maintain contact.

After three years in Edinburgh prison, Sinclair was put on to the 'Training for Freedom' programme, a scheme designed to ease the passage from life in prison to life back in the community. During this time, Sinclair was allowed periods of home leave and he would stay with his mother at her new house in Bellfield Street in the east end of Glasgow.

There are no official records of the decision-making processes that led to his eventual release but it is clear that, when he walked free from jail in 1968, a very dangerous man was being allowed back on to the streets. It is worth reflecting on the facts that are known about his release from custody because they raise serious issues that still confront us today and are yet to be satisfactorily resolved.

All those involved with Sinclair at this time gave the same bleak assessment of his character. He was judged to be a liar who posed a risk for the foreseeable future. As he served that first custodial sentence, it became apparent that he had shallow emotions and no remorse for his crime. This was apparently seen by some as normal because of his age and the length of time he'd been behind bars. In retrospect, it seems more like an excuse rather than a reason and I would question these factors as a satisfactory explanation for someone's apparent inability to see anything wrong with killing a seven-year-old girl during a violent sexual assault.

Rather than prioritising his emotions and the likelihood of him reoffending, those holding the key to his cell seem to have been more concerned about his ability to find work on the outside and perhaps their pragmatism is understandable. After all, here was a young man who had already come under negative influences so they must have deemed it best to get him out of that environment sooner rather than later – and he had developed skills. In the jail in Aberdeen, prisoners could work for a well-established business that made fishing nets for the city's trawler fleet. Sinclair had worked in the net workshop for some time and had become adept at knot tying. This was something that would be of great interest to us later in the investigation.

Overall, it is clear he managed to keep out of serious trouble though senior prison officers concluded this was largely due to his cunning and his ability to avoid getting caught and to work the system. During his first experience of jail, he had already adapted well to the loss of freedom. His future spells behind bars would see him continue in the same way and become the adaptable model prisoner.

Edinburgh prison in those days ran one of Scotland's main 'Training for Freedom' programmes and many prisoners heading for release spent time at Saughton, as it's known, learning a trade that could give them a chance to go into the outside world and earn a living. Sinclair took a painting and decorating course and obtained City & Guilds qualifications. Under the TFF programme, he would leave prison each morning to work on the outside and return to his cell at night. His first job was with an Edinburgh city-centre firm of painters and decorators and so, with supreme irony, Angus Sinclair was first introduced to Edinburgh via the criminal justice system. He got to know the town while training for freedom – who knows how the future may have turned out had he been released from another prison? The law of unintended consequences can surely never have had a more catastrophic outcome.

The dire warnings of all those years before were obviously beginning to fade from memory and the main problem facing Sinclair, by now twenty-two years old, as far as the authorities were concerned, was to get him into sustainable employment. The thinking behind this drive was simply that a man with an income is less likely to reoffend than one who has no stable home and job. It is as true today as it was then. However, although it is generally true, it is less relevant for some offenders than it is for others. In fact, it would later be revealed that after his release, in the very first weeks out of jail, he had sex with a girl he knew to be only fifteen, fully aware that it was against the law.

The painting company that Sinclair worked for while he was training for freedom offered him a full-time job on his release and so he began work proper. He became friendly with other decorators employed by the firm. One in particular was a man who lived just off the High Street in Edinburgh – a few yards from the World's End – and Sinclair visited him at his home as their friendship blossomed.

Sinclair was under a supervision order for three years after his release. During the time he was being supervised, he was in regular contact with probation officers and we discovered he'd had a number of girlfriends. Some of these women were traced and interviewed. They told us how Sinclair had bought a small van and he used to take some of them for runs in it throughout Edinburgh and into the neighbouring county of East Lothian, past the spots where Helen and Christine's bodies would be found years later.

Eventually Sinclair entered into a more stable relationship with a nice girl, a student nurse he had met in Edinburgh. Just a month after his twenty-fifth birthday, he married the girl. She was called Sadie Hamilton but everyone knew her as Sarah. Eighteen months later, Sinclair became a father when Sarah gave birth to a son. The couple had, by this time, left Edinburgh and moved back to Glasgow, home city to both of them. They set up home in Nitshill. It was a good start – a steady job, a child and their own house – but married life for Mr and Mrs Sinclair was anything but smooth. The five-foot-two painter and decorator soon started a string of affairs during their early married life – at least six. This led to periods of separation and, during one of them, he moved in with another woman. Despite this, Sarah felt they had a fairly normal married life.

She knew he had been in jail but was not fully aware of the nature of his crimes until many years later. She certainly had no knowledge of the fact that her husband, whilst supposedly out with friends or on fishing trips, had become a violent predatory criminal engaged in a frenzy of offending in the late 1970s.

When he eventually made his next court appearance, this time at Scotland's highest criminal court, the High Court in Edinburgh, in the summer of 1982, Sinclair admitted eleven charges of rape and indecency involving eleven girls, ranging in age from six to fourteen, but denied assaulting a boy of nine. His rape victims were aged just eight, ten and fourteen. The other girls had all been subjected to terrifying ordeals, over a considerable length of time, that must have left them in a state of shock which I imagine will live with them still. The simple recitation of these facts cannot begin to give even the slightest indication of the suffering Sinclair caused to these unfortunate children and their families.

Each offence was similar. The girls were attacked in the entrances or closes of tenement blocks, either the one they lived in or one near their home. Each time he deployed the same methods. He enticed the girls into these often dark and deserted passageways by stopping them in the street and asking for directions or asking them to run an errand for him in exchange for money – exactly the same ruse as he had used in the killing of Catherine Reehill.

Reading all of this years later, it once again highlights a fundamental flaw in our criminal justice system. It is this – we can have someone clearly marked out as a high-risk individual who has been subjected to all sorts of reports, examinations and assessments, most of which offer dire predictions as to his likely future behaviour, and, despite it all, he is freed into the community to commit the very acts all those who had contact with him knew he was capable of and indeed likely to perpetrate. Nowhere was there the procedure to intercede or prevent what was for so many people a plainly foreseeable result.

During Operation Trinity, we would question why he had switched from the adult victims of 1977 to children but, regardless of the age of the victims, he was an offender who worked to an established modus operandi – he was a creature of habit, organisation and remorseless resolve. The alleged offence against the boy didn't fit his usual pattern but, because he admitted the other charges, it was allowed to remain on file. We will never know for sure but, even if it was Sinclair who attacked the boy, he would have been unlikely to admit it. In the twisted logic of some sex offenders, there is a world of difference between sex attacks on females of any age and boys. It may simply have been a matter of preserving his own self-image – his honour.

Before his arrest, these attacks on children had been widely reported in the local press but investigating officers had not publicly linked them. The widespread press coverage given to his court appearance meant that few inmates of Glasgow's Barlinnie Jail would have been unaware of his crimes when he joined their ranks on 30 August 1982. The judge at Sinclair's trial, Lord John Cameron, was famous for his tough, no-nonsense approach to criminals and he had been one of the last judges in Scotland to pass the death penalty. He sentenced Sinclair to life, recommending he serve at least fifteen years but adding the rider that, in Sinclair's case, he thought life should mean exactly that.

Being jailed as an adult paedophile offender was a tough lesson for the diminutive Sinclair. Despite his constant workouts in the jail gym and a near obsession with fitness routines, he had been given a thorough beating by fellow prisoners on at least two occasions within weeks of his arrival in prison just after he was sentenced. After that, he was content to remain a protected prisoner under the rules designed to save sex offenders from inmates' jail justice. Even at Peterhead Prison's sex offenders unit, where he was by the time Operation Trinity had started, Sinclair's fear of retribution from other prisoners remained with him. It was known that he did not relish a move back to the relatively unprotected environment of the general prison population.

As we progressed with the inquiry, we did sometimes reflect that this fear of being put back into the mainstream might work in our favour. The time would inevitably come when Sinclair would have to be formally questioned. This would be a lengthy process lasting for several days and may require Sinclair to be moved to a prison more convenient for this purpose. We hoped, somewhere at the back of our minds, that he would be so keen to stay within his comfort zone at Peterhead that he may decide to make a clean breast of it all and give us a full voluntary confession. He had, on some occasions, been quite forthcoming in the past and been able to admit his guilt but only when it was clear there was a compelling case against him and it was in his interests to do so. Any confession he made had been as a pragmatic response to a hopeless situation – when he thought he had a chance, he admitted nothing.

It became increasingly apparent that the picture we were forming in our minds of the 2004 version of Sinclair was of a completely different person to the one jailed twenty years earlier. He seemed somehow to have reinvented himself and it was as though he believed there was no connection between this trusted, organised key figure in the smooth running of Peterhead Prison's kitchen and the sordid offender that had done so much harm to innocent children. For him to admit his guilt in these killings, it would mean he would have to give up this self-deception and confront the demons of his past. It didn't seem likely but only time would tell. He would know that, one day in the not too far distant future, he would be speaking to us. Until that day arrived, it was not possible for us to predict what sort of reception we would get.

It was certain that, no matter what happened, we needed a clear and sophisticated strategy to make sure we got the best out of these eventual interviews. There would be no second chances. A key part of the success of the inquiry would be to carry out detailed profiling

Top Left Anna Kenny – disappeared on 5 August 1977, but her body was not found until 23 April 1979.

Top Right Mary Gallagher – murdered on 19 November 1978. Her size gave her an almost child-like appearance. Angus Sinclair was convicted of her murder in 2001.

Left Matilda McAuley – a hard working mother killed on 2 October 1977.

Above Agnes Cooney – a warm and caring girl. She was killed on 3 or 4 December 1977.

Left to Right Helen Scott and Christine Eadie, on either side of a friend. This picture was taken shortly before their deaths.

The World's End lounge bar – October 1977.

Above. The World's End lounge bar – October 1977.

Left. Artist's impression of the typical 70s dress style of the men last seen with Helen and Christine.

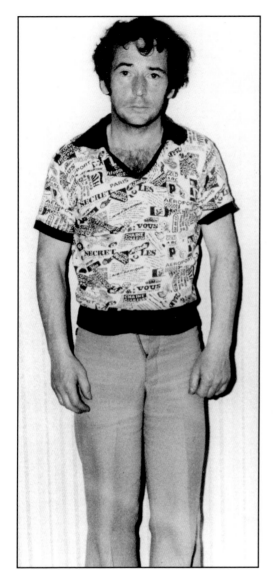

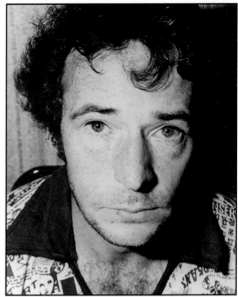

Above Angus Sinclair: a small but powerfully built man.

Top Right Angus Sinclair as he looked in 1982 when he was arrested for a series of rapes and assaults on children.

Right Gordon Hamilton, an enigma of a man who left little behind to mark his life. This was the best picture we could trace.

Above Helen and Christine – the best of pals and hardly more than girls. Ultimately they were denied justice.

Far Left Helen Scott.

Left Christine Eadie.

The early Edinburgh Incident Room. The clutter of paperwork and files seem alien by today's computerised standards. DC Stuart Hay, nearest the camera, DS David 'Yogi' Brunton and DC Eric Bowman still did a fine job. *SCRAN.*

Near the deposition site of Christine Eadie, October 1977. Primitive scenes of crime techniques by today's standards – no tape or barrier to protect the scene were used at the time. *SCRAN.*

Above Searches at the deposition site of Helen Scott, haphazard by today's standards – no protective clothing and the lack of a systematic approach makes this a scene from a bygone age. *SCRAN*.

Right Early publicity for the investigation. Detective Constable John Capaldi, a stalwart of the early enquiry, stands to the right. *SCRAN*.

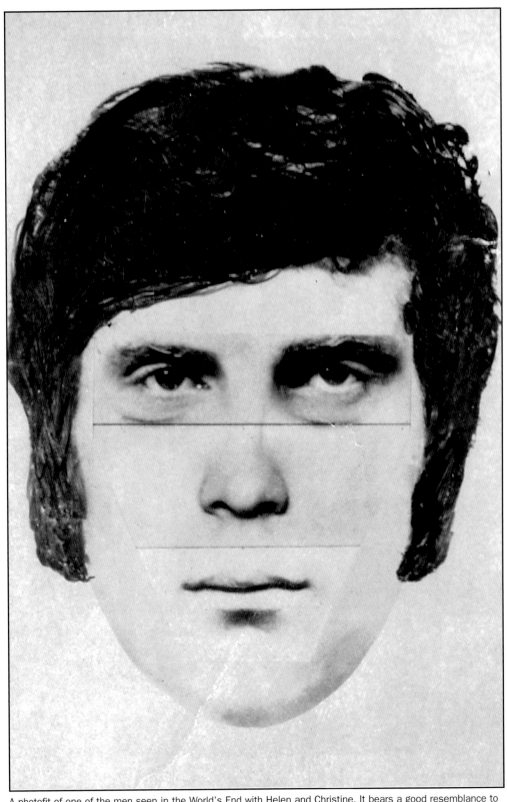

A photofit of one of the men seen in the World's End with Helen and Christine. It bears a good resemblance to both Angus Sinclair and Gordon Hamilton.

Right A reconstruction of the last known movements of Helen and Christine. Police cadets took the role of the girls.

Below The actual Toyota caravanette owned and used by Angus Sinclair at the time of the World's End murders. We traced all its subsequent owners but found it had been scrapped a few months before our enquiry re-opened.

Left Eddie Cotogno – associate of Angus Sinclair. His death is still a mystery.

Is this sick sex beast the World's End killer?

LINKS TO JAILED MANIAC, HIS ASSOCIATE AND BIZARRE MURDER OF PHOTOGRAPHER

They're the murders that sickened a nation. Women victims killed by men they may never have met before and who escaped justice. Seven Glasgow prostitutes murdered in the past six years are just the latest in a series of unsolved murders. Today, the Scottish Mirror re-opens the files.

VICTIMS OF THE LADYKILLERS

Above Right Press speculation made the links, just as we did.

Above The World's End as it is today – a popular tourist pub, just as it was in 1977.

Right Tom Wood.

Above The best at their best. Detective Superintendent Ian Thomas and Detective Chief Inspector Allan Jones. Their persistence closed the case.

Right Angus Sinclair – murderer, rapist and paedophile. He has now been in prison for 34 of his 60 years.

of Sinclair to allow the officers who would eventually be tasked with interviewing him to know their man. They needed to be able to build some sort of bridge to his thinking, to quickly establish a relationship which could allow them to get to the truth.

Perhaps unusually against this background of sexual crime, Sinclair's wife stayed in some sort of contact with him – not to any great extent but, after a few years, she even began visiting him from time to time. Sarah and their son had, by this time, moved to the south of England so the journey to remote Peterhead would have been a long and difficult one.

Not long after his arrival at Peterhead Sinclair had sought entry to the prison's sex offenders programmes to seek help in overcoming his offending behaviour. We found this particularly interesting because it was a classic example of split personality. On the one hand, Sinclair was a model prisoner, a trusty with the run of large parts of the jail including the administrative offices. The prison officers had faith in him and he, in turn, had never let them down. Yet, at the same time, there was a very different and dangerous persona in Sinclair. It was concluded that Sinclair was an extremely cold and callous person and still showed not a shred of remorse for his crimes. More worryingly still, he had not changed at all during his sentence. He was dangerous and manipulative.

So as one group of professionals were assessing Sinclair as devious and dangerous, others who worked with him day to day saw him in an entirely different light as a trusty, hard-working and reliable individual – a model prisoner in every way.

It was at this time when we first learned that Sinclair had spoken of being a victim of sexual abuse himself. This is interesting because, as is well known, there is often a link between being a victim of sexual abuse and a perpetrator of the same or similar types of crime. Whether this was true or not, we will never know but one facet of Sinclair's character was clearly emerging – his devotion to his duties in the prison and his ability as a painter and decorator both pointed to a need for approval. He was a perfectionist because it was a route to self-worth and esteem. A complex character was emerging – one the one hand, he was violent man, a thief and a sexual predator who exercised power over women by extreme violence and, on the other, he was a perfectionist and a hard worker who sought approval and status by his labours. Angus Sinclair was two very different people but to what extent did he realise it? Was he in control of both sides of his character and where did the fault line lie?

The analysis of Sinclair was important but we had practicalities to consider. What was quite clear to us was the fact that, whilst he may well not have been a model husband by virtue of his affairs, he does not appear to have been committing sexual offences during the early years of his married life. In fact, until 1977, when he was having difficulties in his relationship with Sarah, he seems to have kept himself under reasonable control. But then, for some reason, the balance changed and there was an explosion of offending that culminated in the horrific catalogue of crimes he admitted to in 1982 and the World's End murders that we were investigating. What the trigger was perhaps even Sinclair does not know. Was it the difficulties at home or were these domestic difficulties being caused by his descent into the depths of paedophilic offending? Was it simply an uncontrollable urge or that he had freedom and opportunity? It was clear that he had offended alone and with an accomplice. What were the factors that influenced that decision?

Whatever the answer to these questions are, one thing was clear – he was still dangerous and experts told us that an accurate assessment of his character was virtually impossible because of his ability to deceive. At times, he was less dangerous than others but he was never safe.

Through the 1990s, Sinclair remained in Peterhead Prison and, despite the view of the judge, Lord Cameron, in 1982 that he should remain in jail for the rest of his natural life, in the spring of 1997, the release process for Sinclair began again. As is routine, reports were compiled to allow decisions to be made and Sinclair, trying his best to appear open, gave some interesting accounts of his earlier behaviour. He said how his life, after his release from that first ten-year sentence for the killing of Catherine Reehill, revolved round home and work. He painted a picture of how he often put in very long hours at his painting jobs and inferred that his only relaxation was occasional fishing trips. He had few friends – particularly relevant for us later in our investigation was the fact that one of them was his wife's brother, Gordon Hamilton. They spent a lot of time together, fishing and making occasional visits to various pubs.

The presentation of Sinclair prior to him being considered for release from the life sentence is perhaps the most telling of all. He would have to demonstrate that he was no longer a risk to society and of course one of the strong indicators of this would be whether or not he had come to realise the full enormity of his crimes and show that he was truly and demonstratively remorseful.

Peterhead Prison pioneered a programme for sex offenders which has won international respect. It aims to get offenders to confront their crimes and realise the dreadful effect they have had on their victims. Bear in mind that this unit in Peterhead is home to the majority of Scotland's most serious and prolific convicted perpetrators of sex crimes. The time he spent on this programme would certainly be one of the main factors that the Parole Board, the body that would ultimately decide on his suitability for release, would have taken into consideration. His first application for parole was declined in 1999, with the board perhaps concluding that Sinclair's lack of empathy towards his victims was an issue. They must also have feared there was still a risk of his reoffending or certainly that the risk of reoffending had not been totally eliminated.

The lack of victim empathy was demonstrated in the extreme by his clear belief that the little girls he targeted in those attacks in the late 1970s were somehow willing participants. One signature of his offending patterns then was that he would give money to those who he attacked and this clearly allowed him to square his conscience and, in his distorted thinking processes, to consider that both parties in the attacks gained something from the experience. Clearly this twisted thinking would have been uppermost in the Parole Board's mind when they turned down his application. It is very common to fail at the first attempt with the Parole Board. The next time, with another year or so of exemplary reports, he would have a better chance.

That chance never came. Forensic science was advancing and Sinclair's past was starting to catch up with him. For the first but not the last time, justice would reach out to Angus Sinclair from beyond the grave.

The brutal sexual murder of diminutive seventeen-year-old Mary Gallagher in Glasgow in November 1978 had been the subject of a major police inquiry with thousands of man hours devoted to attempting to track down her killer. Her body was found on waste ground near a railway station in the Springburn area of the city.

The case, while still open and under investigation, had long since been on a back burner after detectives concluded they had explored every possible line of inquiry. Then, in the spring of 2000, officers received credible information, naming a specific individual as Mary's killer. The person named by their informant was not Sinclair. The lead was positive and it came from a reliable source so the inquiry was reopened and a new investigation began into the named suspect, who had not featured in the original inquiry and who I will not name here for reasons that will become obvious.

The inquiry progressed some distance with information being gathered on their new suspect's background and movements with the eventual aim of arresting him at some point in the near future and questioning him over the allegation. As part of that inquiry, old productions, that is to say evidence from the crime scene, were routinely sent for further forensic examination and DNA testing and, because of the very advances in that science that were to serve us so well later, a perfect DNA profile was obtained. It was clear there was no link between the preserved evidence from the Mary Gallagher crime scene and the new suspect. However, there was a perfect match with the DNA profile of someone already on the national database – Angus Robertson Sinclair. Officers quickly checked through their files and discovered that, in the huge database of suspects – thousands of names – he had not featured in the original inquiry.

Mary Gallagher's body was found on waste ground. She had been walking across the waste ground with an eleven-year-old local boy. He had run off after their progress was halted by a man standing at the side of the road staring at them. Even though twenty-three years had intervened, that boy, now a man, was able to look across the High Court in Edinburgh from the witness box to the dock and identify Sinclair as the man he saw that day as he was walking with Mary. He said how, as a child, he had been terrified of the man's staring eyes. 'He had eyes like dark holes,' he said.

The jury, or at least a majority of them, concluded that such was the terror of the eleven-year-old that he was still able to recall accurately the eyes even two decades later as he looked at the greying man with those penetrating eyes now behind gold-rimmed spectacles. The DNA match of course was more powerful still and Sinclair was again sentenced to life imprisonment.

So, by 2001, it was clear that there was more to Sinclair's offending than had been thought. The horrific attacks on the children had been preceded by the murder of Mary Gallagher. The obvious question to ask was what other crimes could he have committed. There were several unsolved murders of young women in the 1970s and several had taken place in Sinclair's area of Glasgow.

The Mary Gallagher trial judge, Lord Carloway, imposed a life sentence, saying he should stay in jail for the rest of his natural life for what he called a 'callous, brutal and depraved act'.

When it happened, the murder of seventeen-year-old Mary had horrified Scotland and, as details of the killing of Mary Gallagher were recounted at the trial, the passage of time before her killer was brought to justice had done nothing to dilute that horror. She had been strangled with the leg of her trousers and then raped.

At this point, it is very pertinent to note that, if Strathclyde Police had not received the tip-off – incorrect though it turned out to be – that led to Sinclair's conviction for this crime, he may well have been released in 2001 instead of standing trial for this crime. There is no indication that the Parole Board would have said he was fit to be freed but certainly the fact that the wheels were being put in motion to start the process that may have ended in his release is significant. His conviction in 2001 ensured that this would not now happen. The judge had made it clear. Sinclair had joined the club of three other killers in Scotland who would never be released from jail.

One other obvious question arises from the Gallagher case – had a false lead not caused the reopening of the case, would Sinclair have escaped justice for Mary's murder? The answer is that for a time he may have but eventually the truth would have emerged. As a consequence of the World's End and a number of other historical cases, police forces are now routinely examining all unsolved cases and subjecting surviving forensic samples to the latest scientific examination. The work of these 'cold case' units will surely bring resolution to some of the country's most notorious unsolved cases in the years to come. Many offenders, including rapists and murderers, will find themselves facing justice many years after they thought they had got away with their crimes. The Mary Gallagher case would have been solved – not in 2001 but eventually.

As soon as Sinclair was convicted and the newspapers were no longer fettered by the contempt of court provisions, they began reporting a new development in the case of Sinclair. They were speculating that he may be responsible for three other murders of young women in the west of Scotland. They detailed the potential victims as twenty-three-year-old Agnes Cooney, thirty-six-year-old Hilda McAuley and twenty-year-old Anna Kenny who were all murdered in 1977. The fact of the matter was that, whilst Sinclair was a prime suspect for these killings, there was no evidence to connect him to them directly.

The furore in the aftermath of the 2001 trial eventually died down and the press speculation faded but it was not the end of interest in Sinclair and speculation as to the unsolved murders. Operation Trinity was to consider all these cases again in 2004 and did so in the most minute detail.

6

The Second Man

But we still hadn't found the second man or rather the first man –
the one whose DNA profile we had identified all these years before
and who we had been searching for ever since. We had spent many
hundreds of man hours and tens of thousands of pounds in targeted
testing, elimination screening and database searches – all to no
avail. It had been a frustrating and a puzzling exercise. Could it be
that our man, the only profile we had identified for years, was a first
offender? Was he dead? Or had he stopped offending before the
practice of taking DNA samples from offenders had been established? We were desperate to find out and now that Angus Sinclair
had been identified as one of the men present on Helen and
Christine's last night we knew we were closing in. We were sure
that the unidentified man must be an associate of Sinclair. It was
logical, the two men last seen with Helen and Christine in the
World's End were obviously together – friends out for the night –
and, while we were not certain that one of them was Sinclair, there
was a very good chance he was. In any case, for two men to have
been involved in such a crime and to have kept silent for all those
years, they must be close.

As in all searches, we started at the centre and worked outwards
and Angus Sinclair was the centre. Using all the techniques available
to us, old and new, we trawled every aspect of Sinclair's life to solve
the puzzle – criminal associates, friends, workmates and relatives.
You might think this would have been a simple enough process

but it involved looking back almost thirty years with no current information as Sinclair had been in prison since 1982. It was to be yet another difficult exercise.

When the man's identity was finally confirmed, he turned out to be someone closer to Angus Sinclair than even we could have hoped or imagined. By a process of elimination, we were able to determine, through testing the Y chromosome from the original unidentified DNA sample from the World's End killings, that it came from the same paternal line as the five brothers of Sarah Hamilton, Angus Sinclair's wife. We eventually established for certain that none of the brothers matched the World's End profile exactly so there were now two possibilities. The man we were looking for was either another sibling of the brothers, the only missing brother Gordon Hamilton, or someone totally unconnected with them.

As so often in cases like this, it came down to a calculation of probabilities. The scientists had to work out what the chances were of the DNA profile recovered from the bodies of Helen and Christine not being that of Gordon Hamilton. In this instance, Dr Jonathan Whitaker, one of the country's foremost DNA experts, was clear – the odds against it being Gordon Hamilton were at least thirty-eight million to one. That is to say, in the careful language of the scientist, there was an extremely strong possibility that Gordon was the source of the sample.

We were now certain that Gordon Hamilton was the second man at the scene of the World's End murders. By a process of elimination, Jonathan Whitaker had followed the familial line of the Hamiltons and concluded, beyond reasonable doubt, that the crime scene samples found in the World's End case must have come from Gordon Hamilton, who had died in 1996.

So, after all those years, there it was – Angus Sinclair had been with his brother-in-law in Edinburgh that night in October 1977. After nearly thirty years, we were sure we had found the two men we were looking for.

To conclude the identification, all we had to do was trace a sample of Gordon's DNA and check it against the crime scene sample – straightforward. Most people leave traces many years after their death, hospital samples, possessions they have touched and left with traces of their DNA, clothes they have worn or even family photographs they have handled during their lives. Depending on climatic conditions, DNA can survive for many years. We thought that, with a systematic approach, we could surely find some earthly trace of Gordon Hamilton – after all, at that time, he had only been dead for eight years. The most obvious option was exhumation of Gordon's body – DNA remains detectable in the body for years especially in bone marrow – but this was quickly ruled out as Gordon had been cremated. Thus began a bizarre, complex and long-running inquiry within an inquiry to track down some remnant of Gordon Hamilton. The search was to intrigue us and frustrate us and it became a fixation for Allan Jones.

Once it became apparent that Gordon's mortal remains were beyond our reach, our next obvious choice was his possessions – a wristwatch perhaps or a piece of jewellery, a cigarette lighter, a wallet, any article that had been his and that we could prove he had handled frequently and left behind. We drew a complete blank – Gordon had left nothing. Neither his wife nor his family had any keepsake that had belonged to Gordon. We then decided to follow the medical route. Gordon had had regular illnesses especially towards the end of his life so perhaps the local hospital had a blood sample or maybe samples had been retained from his post-mortem examination. We could find nothing. It was as if all traces of Gordon Hamilton had been erased – as if he had never existed.

By this time the search for a trace of Gordon Hamilton was becoming a personal challenge for the team and in particular Allan Jones. It will be already apparent that Allan doesn't give up easily and he wasn't about to now. We had obviously been doing extensive background checks into Gordon's life ever since his

DNA had identified him as one of the killers. We knew he was a strange man, arrogant and bombastic, opinionated, abrasive on occasions yet withdrawn, private and reclusive in other areas of his life. He had been a difficult man to assess – even his brothers and sisters could not paint a vivid picture of him. We even had difficulties getting a photograph of him until we eventually got hold of a faded family snap from his sister's photograph album.

However, we did know something about his work. He had been good with his hands and, from time to time, he did little jobs for friends and relatives – just basic electrical work and painting and decorating. As a last resort, Allan Jones and his team pursued this line of inquiry with vigour. We learned that he had carried out some electrical work in a house in Glasgow some years before he died. He had wired some bedroom lights for a friend and this had entailed leading electrical cable behind a bedroom wall. This could be just the break we needed. If Gordon had handled the cables and the cables had been sealed behind the wall since that time, it was possible that he had left traces of his DNA.

Allan and his team found the house, got permission from the owners and recovered what we thought might be the cabling but to no avail – no DNA traces could be found. The hunt continued when we learned that Gordon had done some home decorating for a relative in Glasgow. We knew for sure that he had wallpapered a room in a flat in the centre of Glasgow and that he had put a polystyrene coving round the edge of the ceiling at the same time. There was little chance of recovering anything from the wallpaper or paint but we thought that he must have handled the coving strips while putting them in place so perhaps somewhere on the coving there was a vestige of Gordon Hamilton.

In what was a last resort, Allan and his team found the house, deftly retrieved the coving, preserved it carefully and sent it to the Wetherby lab. Swabs were taken and to our delight traces of DNA were found. The sample was tiny but it was enough to make a match with the profile from the World's End sample. At last we had found Gordon Hamilton.

It all sounds fairly simple, even mundane, when written down. That conclusion, though, was the end product of scientific endeavour going back to the day Helen and Christine's bodies were found. At various times, it involved work at the very cutting edge of science. The truth hiding in those samples had been elusive. Witnessing how DNA technology has evolved and helped us, just as it has the entire criminal detection process the world over, was one of the more fascinating parts of Operation Trinity.

But we still had much to do. We had identified Gordon Hamilton as one of our suspects but we knew little of him. He was long dead and although he was known to the authorities it was for minor scrapes with the law. We quickly learned that his relationship with alcohol had killed him prematurely but apart from that we knew almost nothing. Importantly we had no firm evidence of the links between Gordon and Angus Sinclair and, evidentially, this was very important.

If we were to prove that a social relationship between Sinclair and his brother-in-law existed, we would need to conduct lengthy and often difficult interviews with surviving members of Gordon's family of ten brothers and sisters. Foremost amongst those was Gordon's sister Sarah, Angus Sinclair's wife. She, more than any of her siblings, knew the details of Sinclair's relationships with members of her family. It should be put on record that her help to our inquiry was unstinting and invaluable and allowed us to progress further and faster than we would have without her assistance.

By any definition of the word it is fair to say that the Hamiltons were a troubled family. The children appeared to have been brought up in terror of their domineering and sometimes violent father, and several of them went through adult life the victims of chronic alcoholism that led to the premature death of several, both male and female. Other siblings were persistent offenders and, as such, not the natural allies of the police.

We now know much more about the genetic inheritance of addictive personalities – the predisposition to become addicted to either alcohol or drugs or both. If one of your parents is addicted you have four times the chance of becoming addicted yourself; if both your parents are addicts you are eight times more likely. The Hamiltons are a tragic example of a family stricken and almost destroyed by addiction – in their case to alcohol.

It is to the credit of surviving members of this family, most of whom had difficult relationships with alcohol, crime or both, that, in the main, they did their best to help us. Despite clearly incriminating himself in the process, one of Sarah's younger brothers volunteered details of the crimes of violence and theft he committed with Angus; these offences were to form an important part of the investigation. He perhaps did not tell us the complete truth about his relationship with Sinclair but he was frank enough to give us some key pointers.

When Operation Trinity was in its early stages we were in the position of being certain that the DNA profile belonged to a member of the Hamilton family but not which one it was. At that time, Gordon Hamilton did not jump out of the family profile as being the most likely candidate for Sinclair's accomplice in killing. According to all who knew him, Sinclair was most friendly with another of Sarah's brothers, who was some six years younger than Sarah. Sarah and her surviving brothers and sisters seemed pretty clear that Gordon and Angus were on little better than nodding terms. The younger brother was by far the best prospect but the chance of him being the second killer was soon eliminated when he provided us with a swab for DNA testing. When the results came back, his DNA clearly did not fit the profile of Sinclair's accomplice and he was ruled out as a suspect.

In trying to build an overall picture of Sinclair's involvement in his wife's family, we attempted to establish just how much the Hamiltons, individually or collectively, knew of his past. Sarah, for instance, knew that he had been in jail but was adamant she did not know anything of the details behind her husband's imprisonment other than perhaps having an inkling about the general type of the offence.

Sarah first got to know the man who was to cause her so much pain and anguish in the years to come in Edinburgh in the late summer of 1969. She was a student nurse and was introduced to Sinclair by a friend of hers who was actually already in a relationship with him. Not long after that, Sinclair and the friend split up and he took up with Sarah. When Sarah and Angus eventually married, her parents were not at the Edinburgh registry office ceremony. She is certain that, in the months after the marriage, when her new husband met his parents-in-law, he got on well with them, but it seems clear Sarah was ever mindful of the trouble she knew would ensue if her father found out about his past jail term, no matter what the nature of the offence had been. This fear was based on Sarah's sketchy knowledge of Sinclair's crimes. One can only imagine the likely reaction of her father if he ever found out the whole truth about his son-in-law – that he was a convicted child killer.

The complicated family relationships of the Hamilton clan were extremely important to us because of the DNA clues that were going to lead to the solution of the World's End killings. It is fair to say Angus Sinclair polarised the Hamilton family. There were those who detested him and went to any length to ensure they had no dealings with him at all. Sarah's brother Thomas, for example, completely forbade his wife to accept lifts with Sinclair even though she was very friendly with Sarah. To Thomas, Sinclair was a 'nonce', prison slang for a sex offender, and, although he had no precise knowledge of his crime, he wanted his family, particularly his wife, to have as little to do with him as possible. However, Sinclair got on very well with another sister-in-law, and it seemed as if they had a close relationship. Somewhere in the middle of this spectrum of emotion and involvement was Gordon. On the face of it, the relationship between Gordon and Angus Sinclair appeared to be little more than a nodding acquaintance – just as other members of the family had described – but, as we were to slowly discover, Gordon was a man with another side to him, a hidden side which was to draw him into a friendship with Sinclair through their shared interests of the darkest kind.

Then there was the younger brother, who had been closest to Sinclair. His lifelong addictions to alcohol and crime have left him in a sorry state – we knew he was suffering from severe medical problems and living alone in London. However, when we tracked him down to the bedsit in the west of the capital where he was living, he was very helpful, especially after the severity and nature of the crimes under investigation were made known to him. Without hesitation, he outlined the kinds of crimes he and Sinclair carried out and he told us about one particularly brutal offence which would become an important part of the jigsaw puzzle. I cannot stress too much the need for the corroboration of scientific evidence. In Scots law, a single source of information is not enough – it has to be backed up by a second corroborative statement in all crimes from the most minor to the most serious. The younger Hamilton told us of a crime, no doubt long forgotten by all except the victims, that gave us a real insight into Sinclair's method of operation, his pattern of offending, and would, we felt sure, tell a lot about the man in the dock. The fact that, by revealing details of this event, he incriminated himself in a serious offence is an indication of how far he was prepared to go to help us.

Heaven knows what John and Elizabeth Black (their names have been changed to protect their identity) must have thought at first when police came knocking on their door apparently fired by an new determination to solve the crime that had been committed against them nearly thirty years before. The horrific nature of what happened to the couple in their then home in the Moodiesburn area of Lanarkshire near Glasgow meant they would not have forgotten the details of what occurred one awful day in April 1976 – even if they thought the police had.

Elizabeth had left her council-owned home in a typical tenement-style block of six flats in Bridgeburn Drive to go to her work in a nearby miners' club. It was Friday morning and the day the rent was due to be paid. Her husband John had stayed in bed after a late shift at the factory where he worked, leaving their daughter in charge of the rent money. She wasn't well that morning and had stayed off school. Her mother had told the seven-year-old exactly what to do when the rent man arrived at his regular time later that morning – nothing could go wrong.

The young girl was watching television when there was a knock on the front door at about 10 a.m. Having no reasons to think that it could be anyone other than the rent man, the little girl opened the door without a second thought only to be greeted by a terrifying sight. Before her stood two men with stockings over their faces – one was carrying a knife, the other a hammer. The taller of the two men dragged the hysterical youngster up the hallway of the house, holding his knife to her throat, whilst the second man burst into her parents' bedroom and threatened a, by now, wide awake John Black with a hammer.

Both were roughly bundled into the living room of the house and made to lie face down on the floor. Quickly the intruders bound the father and daughter's arms and feet with Sellotape and both were gagged using the same material. They were then left alone as Sinclair and Hamilton waited for the rent man in another room in the house. Sure enough, before long, there was a knock at the door and the shout of 'Rent man!' Mr Black could hear a violent struggle as the rent man was overpowered. Mr Black clearly heard the attackers demanding the keys to the safe rent collectors kept in their vehicles. Then silence.

A short time passed and the taller man came back into the living room and thrust a bundle of notes towards Mr Black saying, 'This is for your troubles – sorry about the inconvenience.'

As the attackers fled with the rent money, John Black was able to break free from his bonds and help his daughter. Then he found the rent collector bound and sitting in a chair in the kitchen. He was bleeding profusely from a head wound and blood was spattered across the floor. Obviously the unfortunate man had been the victim of a level of violence that was far in excess of what most criminals would have thought necessary to inflict.

By telling us this incriminating story in the detail that he did, Sinclair's brother-in-law left himself open to prosecution. However, the Crown Office decided that, in the circumstances and due to the long passage of time, it would not be in the public interest to put him in the dock for this offence, grave as it had been.

The incident was important to us because of the insight it gave into Sinclair's character. It showed his ruthless use of a level of violence that was completely disproportionate to what might have been necessary for the crime he was committing. Sinclair had taken a hammer to the rent collector to subdue him and roughly bound and gagged John Black and his daughter just because he'd had the desire to do so.

Ironically, another man was arrested for the attack. Not long after the incident happened, he was picked out at an identification parade and subsequently put on trial. Thankfully, however, he was acquitted because he had a cast-iron alibi.

Although his brother-in-law spoke about many of the other offences he had committed with Sinclair, it was the robbery of the Moodiesburn rent man that he covered in the most detail. Just as important as Sinclair's appetite for violence was Hamilton's account of his capacity to remain unaffected by the use of such extreme brutality. Having terrified a father and his seven-year-old daughter and committed a vicious attack on the rent collector, Sinclair appeared back where he should have been, minutes later –

on his painting job. He was perfectly calm and controlled, giving nothing away.

Sinclair had been working alongside his brother-in-law just round the corner from the flat when he happened to pick up two bits of information that led to him forming a plan to rob the rent man. He was told you could set your watch by the movements of the rent collector and then, in a different context, he learned that John Black would be at home and in bed after his night shift. Sinclair and Hamilton had put down their brushes, left the job and then, after Sinclair had carried out the violent attack, the pair returned. Sinclair was so unaffected by what he'd done that, to their workmates, it must have seemed for all the world as if they had just popped out for a sandwich.

This information gave us a fascinating insight to the mind and working methods of Angus Sinclair – methods and behaviours that spanned the range of his offending, criminal and sexual, over all his years of freedom.

But we still had much to learn about Gordon Hamilton and his bizarre connections with some of the other crimes we were investigating.

7

Family Ties

Sarah Sinclair has had to bear three great misfortunes in her life. None of them were of her own making but, despite all her troubles, she has always maintained her dignity and tried her best to help us where she could. Above all, she has needed to protect the new life she has created for herself after separating from Sinclair and the nightmare of the old one. Spouses and families of notorious criminals are in a hellish position. At first there is a natural denial on their part, fostered by an instinct for self-preservation and the knowledge that the conviction of a family member can also bring disaster to all those they are closest to. Sometimes there is complicity that stops short of actual participation but is dangerous nonetheless. The desire for self-preservation can shield a relative's eyes to the obvious and leave them unwilling to ask the most basic questions for fear of what the answer would bring. As young detectives, we were always told that alibis provided by wives and mothers were never to be weighed heavily. Throughout our contact with Sarah, she convinced us that she was trying her utmost to deal with a difficult situation as best she could.

Many will be surprised that this nurse, who now lives in the south of England and has had nothing to do with Sinclair for many years, remains married to him. The fact is that, while it is clear their marriage ended in all but name many years before, she has simply never got round to divorcing him. Just why a woman who has done so much to build a new life in a different part of the world would remain married to such a man puzzled my team for a considerable period of time – until they got to know Sarah during many hours of interviews.

From the outset of this inquiry, it was obvious that Sarah Sinclair would be a key to the successful outcome of our investigation. The many years that had passed since the commission of these crimes and the need to establish corroboration for all the evidence eventually to be laid before the court meant that we would have to go into minute detail examining every aspect of Sinclair's past, and Sarah would be able to help us more than most other people that had walked through his life. From the outset, we realised the importance of keeping Sarah on our side. However, it was also clear that recalling the everyday details of her married life twenty-five or more years ago was going to be a very tough task. That those details were bound up in memories of what for anyone could only be described as a traumatic time would make the recall as painful as it was difficult. To her great credit and despite having to deal with what must have been conflicting emotions, Sarah devoted a great deal of time and energy to helping us right from the start and there's no doubt that this must have been a draining commitment for her.

The fact that Sinclair led such a secretive, compartmentalised life allowed him to commit serious offences and kill yet leave many of those closest to him clueless as to the extent of his crimes. When he went off for one of his weekend painting jobs, Sarah had no reason to believe he wasn't doing what he said he was and working away as a painter and decorator. At worst, she may have suspected he was pursuing one of his many affairs but she would certainly have had no idea that he was carrying out the crimes that would be all over the newspapers in the days after he returned home.

Sarah or Sadie Hamilton was just nineteen when she met, fell in love with and married the man she knows as Gus. She was vaguely aware of the fact that Gus had been in jail before their marriage but she didn't know why and, in fact, did not find out for some time after the wedding. When eventually she discovered the awful truth and confronted her husband with the details of what she had found out, he admitted he had, as he put it, 'murdered a child'. For her part, Sarah found herself prepared to give him the benefit of the doubt and make allowances for his young age at the time of the crime. The man she married must have managed to project a very different image from what one would expect of a child killer.

Despite making allowances for his earlier behaviour, Sarah quickly realised that Gus Sinclair was a nightmare of a husband. Serially unfaithful and occasionally violent, he'd get involved in theft, often executed with extreme violence, and he was totally unreliable. Sarah made that assessment based solely on the activities she knew about at the time or had cause to suspect.

It seemed clear to the team who had dealings with Sarah Sinclair that her life has very much been divided into two parts. She was born into straitened circumstances and raised in a dysfunctional family whose lives were largely dominated by petty crime and drink. She'd had a difficult childhood by any standard. From early on, however, Sarah seems to have been determined to put that behind her and strike out on a different course through life from the one that seemed preordained for her. The route she eventually took certainly diverged markedly from the one followed by the rest of her brothers and sisters.

As we have seen, it would appear that Angus Sinclair's major personality traits include deviousness and the total lack of concern for the victims of his crimes. We were keen to learn how these characteristics manifested themselves to someone close to him, so who better to help us with this than his wife?

During his time of offending through the second half of 1977, she had not one iota of a suspicion that her husband might be guilty of the crimes that shocked the country and had everyone talking about them. Each of those killings in Scotland's Central Belt generated immense publicity and none more so than the World's

End murders. Years later, all who knew him at that time who we were able to trace were certain that Sinclair showed no outward signs of any involvement in the crimes. He seemed perfectly normal and at one with himself. It was as though he must have been able to kill in the most bestial and depraved way and, by the time he was back home with his family, behave in what passed for a perfectly normal manner. The capacity to conceal what was going on from those closest to him may seem astounding but it is not uncommon in criminals who disassociate their crimes with the rest of their lives. They compartmentalise their lives as a defence mechanism and to normalise their existence.

From the Word's End murders in the autumn of 1977 to the 1979 murder of Mary Gallagher and through to the sex attacks on children in the next decade, Sinclair had been murdering young women and then raping children. This meant that, in the Central Belt of Scotland between 1977 and June 1982, he had been committing these most brutal of crimes on a regular basis yet Sinclair was managing to appear perfectly normal to those around him. On top of this appalling list of sexual offences, there were also crimes of dishonesty and violence. Carrying on this kind of lifestyle required highly developed organisational skills – in fact the very sort of skills that would lead to his position of trust running the kitchens of Peterhead Prison in later life. In the nineteenth century, Robert Louis Stevenson famously embodied the split personality in his characters Dr Jekyll and Mr Hyde. For a prime example of the split personality in the twentieth century, Angus Robertson Sinclair fits the bill.

Sarah and Gus had many periods of separation, each one coming in the wake of her discovering his latest affair. Each time, he would talk his way back into the marital home with Sarah relenting because of a mixture of her feelings for him and a strong desire to do the best for their son.

At our headquarters even we, a fairly hardened group of

detectives, wondered about this skill in appearing normal despite the horrors that he must have been carrying in his mind. How it could be possible for someone to behave in such a manner and show no outward signs? If you measure his crimes purely in terms of numbers, Sinclair is by no means the worst killer in recent British criminal history. However, the sheer concentration of offending is most unusual. The number of victims, women and children, whose lives he ended or left devastated and the grief and anguish inflicted on their friends and families can scarcely be imagined. That he was able to get away with it undetected for so long has to be a matter of concern for everyone.

Often crimes like the ones we were dealing with here are solved after a tip-off from a member of the offender's circle after a slip-up by the perpetrator, a shared confidence to ease a troubled mind or a change of behaviour so out of character as to cause suspicion. The way Sinclair appears to have been able to shut details of his crimes from his mind and control his emotions meant he gave nothing away even to those closest to him.

The officers in my team were completely certain that, if Sarah Sinclair had had even a suspicion of what her Gus was doing on his weekends and evenings away, she would have had not the least hesitation in reporting him to the police. If only he had given her that suspicion, if only his guard had slipped even slightly, we were convinced she would have ended it there and then. Sad to say but Sinclair did not give Sarah that opportunity.

When Sinclair was arrested on 7 June 1982, accused of the series of child sex crimes, the effect on his wife was devastating. Their son was eleven at the time, an age when he would have been old enough have been aware of the general circumstances and enormity of what was going on.

The months between Sinclair's arrest in June 1982 and his sentencing at the High Court in August of that year are the last time Sarah had any real interaction with her husband. It was during what would have been one of their last conversations that Sinclair uttered a sentence to Sarah that leads me to believe he may have many more crimes to answer for.

He was on remand to Barlinnie Prison in Glasgow awaiting trial, no doubt passing time reflecting on his likely defence. It is not in his devious nature to admit wrongdoing. Sarah had other ideas and we know that she told him in no uncertain terms that, if he was guilty of the child sex charges he was accused of, he should make a clean breast of it. She told Sinclair straight that she did not want to be dragged along with their son into what would undoubtedly be a horrific trial featuring days of little children giving the most distressing evidence. She also expressed to him her growing fear that he may be responsible for other crimes he had not so far been caught for. Sarah must have been worried, knowing what she did about his past, that he may even have killed other children.

In the visiting hall of Barlinnie, Gus was challenged and urged to admit his guilt to save his family and victims from the ordeal ahead. Somewhere in the words that followed Gus did exactly that, saying he was indeed guilty of the offences outlined in the charges. He then added that no one yet knew the scale or scope of his crimes. These references haunt all who have had dealings with Sinclair as well as the relatives of the many females that went missing during the years Sinclair was free to stalk the streets of central Scotland, never to be seen or heard of again. It is likely that we will never know the true extent of his crimes and how many victims, dead and alive, that he left in his wake during that time in the late 70s.

While we carried out a detailed examination of all unsolved murders of women in Scotland, there is still the massive grey area of missing persons. It chills me to read words like 'May have gone away with boyfriend' or 'Believed to have run away to London' which often conclude missing persons reports – they constitute a guess, albeit an educated one, but nevertheless they represent a life being written off in a vague sentence and a haze of uncertainty.

Family Ties

The second of Sarah Sinclair's tragedies is, of course, the fact that her brother Gordon was, for at least part of the time, her husband's partner in crime. The strange thing about this partnership is that it would seem Sinclair and Gordon Hamilton did not appear to be particularly friendly or at least that was the impression they gave. They certainly did not have the close, protective relationship that one might expect joint perpetrators of such serious crimes to have. I suppose it could be that knowledge of the crimes they shared did as much to keep them apart as bring them together. It is extremely hard to imagine the relationship that could exist between two human beings involved in such dreadful crimes. Would they, when alone, go over the details of the World's End killings, reliving the satisfaction they derived from the murders, or would they blank it from their minds and never discuss the events of that night? To rationalise in some way beyond the comprehension of most normal people such behaviour may have been the way they dealt with it. Whatever they did, neither gave an inkling to those closest to them.

Investigators always think it is in their favour when two people are involved in one crime. There are many ways this can be a distinct advantage. They may fall out and one turns so-called Queen's evidence against the other in the hope of a lesser sentence. With two suspects, you have twice the chance of something being inadvertently given away during interview.

There is a basic human compulsion to talk about matters that may be weighing heavily on your mind but, as far as we could discover, neither Angus Sinclair nor Gordon Hamilton ever disclosed what took place between them. Hamilton, of course, took his secrets to the grave with him when he succumbed to the effects of his family's curse of alcoholism in 1996.

Whilst we may never know the exact nature of the relationship between Gordon Hamilton and his brother-in-law, one thing is clear – there was bad feeling within the Hamilton family towards both of them. Gordon Hamilton was found by many to be pompous and overbearing. There was little contact between Gordon and his parents and siblings after he had left the family home. The family was aware that Gordon had married but beyond that they knew little about him. In fact, such was the distance between Gordon and the rest of the family that, even after Angus Sinclair's arrest, they remained oblivious to many details of his life until our officers made them aware of what had been going on.

Before Gus was detained over the sex attacks on children, he and Gordon would occasionally spend weekends together. They'd say they were going fishing and, while they were away, they'd live in the caravanette Angus had bought – a vehicle that was to play such an important part in the Word's End murders. We learned that, despite these lengthy trips away, Angus never brought home any fish – at the time, this would have seemed insignificant but, in hindsight, it was suspicious. These were sensitive issues and, during the early part of Operation Trinity, we were not able to tell Sarah Sinclair of the scope of our inquiries or where they were heading.

Gordon's partnership with Sinclair posed us a further problem. It was simply that Sinclair had the best kind of co-accused – a dead one. We felt certain he would at best try to minimise his part in the crimes. We believed that even he would find it hard to explain the presence of his DNA – especially in the locations it was found in the World's End case – but, despite this, he and his lawyers were certain to try. He would blame Gordon Hamilton for everything he could and cast himself as the minor assistant. Gordon would always be a convenient scapegoat.

It would be some way down the prosecution process before his legal advisers would have total disclosure of the evidence of the case in order for that sort of tactic to be deployed. This possibility underlined the need for the interviews we would conduct with Sinclair to be the most carefully planned and executed encounters that would leave nothing to chance, no holes to be wriggled through at a later date. It was unlikely that Sinclair would say much when being questioned but we had to establish enough for him to show the falseness of potential defences that would be certain to be conjured up at any future trial. In the event, we never got the chance.

We did not think that Sinclair would try to blame Gordon Hamilton right away. For a start, he wouldn't know that we knew about Gordon until the evidence was disclosed and he would certainly not wish to voluntarily lead us to an area in which he may have thought himself vulnerable. We were even uncertain as to whether Sinclair knew that Gordon was dead. More importantly, Sinclair could not have been unaware of the extent of our evidence – especially the DNA profiles.

As we gave thought to these matters, I expect our suspect did as well. Sinclair had a good understanding of DNA technology – after all, it was what had brought him to justice for the Mary Gallagher killing at the very time he thought he was heading for parole and freedom. He must have spent many hours in his Peterhead cell wondering and worrying about what other forensic productions may be lying in laboratories and police storage cupboards waiting to be discovered and bring about the next stage in his downfall. With increasingly sophisticated DNA analysis and cold case reviews taking place across the country, many offenders who had thought they have got away with their crimes may well have cause to think again.

This is where our contact with Sinclair's family became invaluable. For them, having to put so much energy into trying to recall the minute details of the life of a man they had long wanted to forget about must have been frustrating and difficult. For Sarah, there was an additional problem impacting on her life. As any mother would be, she was desperate to protect her son who, by this time, was a young man.

Over many hours of interviews, from the moment her husband was arrested in 1982 right up to and especially during the preparation of the World's End case, Sarah did all she could to help us.

As various matters took on a new urgency or importance, she would be reinterviewed again and she'd always do her very best to recall details of often apparently insignificant events that, twenty-five years on, were now important to us. Details of cars owned by Gus and how long he had driven them for were hard to recall but the information was vital to us. These recall sessions would be even more difficult for her as she had clearly put such a lot of energy into putting her life in Scotland behind her and building a new world far removed from the tough areas of Glasgow where she was brought up and spent so much of her tortured married life with Gus.

One of the other key relationships in Angus Sinclair's life was with Sarah's younger brother. He had lived with them for a while and we learned that during that time he had been involved with Angus in a variety of crimes.

This Hamilton brother was forty-eight years old when we tracked him down to a bedsit in London. We first spoke to him at the time it had become clear from the DNA evidence that the second World's End killer was certainly a member of the Hamilton family – maybe himself and, if not him, certainly one of his brothers. We were still gathering DNA samples from the surviving siblings so there was always going to be the chance that this man was Sinclair's partner in crime. In fact, when he realised how serious the crimes in our inquiries actually were, he was open and candid in a way we might not have expected from someone of his background. It soon became clear that he was indeed a partner in crime with Sinclair but not the crimes we were most interested in. During the time he was staying with his sister Sarah and brother-in-law Gus, the young man had become deeply involved with Sinclair and his violent robberies.

Sinclair had managed to get his young brother-in-law a job with the painting company he worked for in Glasgow and we learned how quite often he and Gus would return at night to office premises where they had been painting by day and steal. These robberies went on undetected for some time. Then Sinclair and the younger Hamilton moved on to till snatches; bursting into a shop or garage and under the threat of violence, or more often with real violence, making off with the contents of the cash register.

As we had learned from the description of the Moodiesburn rent man robbery, the level of violence used was extreme and we discovered that Sinclair's favoured tactic was to take a hammer to the head of his victim without threat or warning. Another particularly horrific example of this occurred in Cumbernauld near Glasgow when Sinclair had attacked a car salesman's daughter who was carrying a relatively large sum of money. Sinclair had lashed out at the terrified woman with the hammer but fled with no money. After they made their escape, Sinclair lost his temper with his accomplice, accusing him of bungling the attack and losing the proceeds.

In another raid on a garage, following information Sinclair had gathered from a prostitute, overwhelming violence was used. Then there was a brutal attack on a man selected at random as he emerged from a pub in Glasgow. In the dark, Sinclair pounced on the man and beat him with the hammer before stealing from his victim seemingly as an afterthought. It was quite clear that Gus was a gratuitously violent man.

But, for all the younger Hamilton appeared to be trying to help and, in doing so, he knew he was incriminating himself in serious offences, the officers who spoke to him felt he was not being entirely frank. There was definitely a suspicion he was holding back – in fact, by checking the stories of other family members, it was quite clear there were areas he was not prepared – or perhaps not able – to go into. I say he may not have been able to tell as much as he might have been because years of alcohol-related illness had taken their toll on his mental faculties. However, it was hard to determine what had been lost from his memory and what was being hidden away at the back of his mind. One thing was sure, though – the DNA evidence from the World's End eventually proved he was not the second man. He was closely related to the second man but it wasn't him.

All in all, the Hamiltons were as helpful as they could be about Gus. It was clear that, while they knew of his involvement in crime, they had no idea of the violent nature of his activities and they certainly had no knowledge of his sexual offending. His wife's strongest indication of Gus's other side came during a police investigation into the strange case of Edward Cotogno. A Glasgow man, he was a clever, able, but seamy individual who used his photographic hobby to deal in home-produced pornography, much of it involving very young local women. He was found dead in the charred remains of his Glasgow home after a fire. He had met a violent end before the fire had been started and police concluded he had been murdered. Extensive inquiries were carried out over many months but no culprit was found. Angus Sinclair and Eddie Cotogno were connected and what happened to Eddie and why remain intriguing parts of this story. At the time of Eddie's death, however, the police knew that Angus Sinclair was one of many of Eddie Cotogno's seedy contacts so he had to be traced, interviewed and eliminated – or become a suspect.

At the time of Cotogno's death, Glasgow detectives were frequently at Gus and Sarah's door wanting to speak to Sinclair because they suspected he was involved in robberies or other crimes about the city. On this particular occasion, they had phoned to make an appointment to see him and Sinclair had straightaway told his wife he though it would be about the death of a man he knew. He said he could not tell the officers where he actually was at the time of the killing for unspecified reasons and asked Sarah to provide a false alibi for him and say he had been at home with her. This she did despite her concerns and fears. Once again, it seems the old rule about not setting too much store by wives' alibis proved true.

We also learned that Sinclair secretly tape-recorded the officers speaking to him, so worried was he about the police investigation. However, we uncovered no hard evidence to connect Sinclair to the death of Eddie Cotogno but the investigation into his murder got close to Gus and that certainly unnerved him.

The more we found out about Sinclair's life from his family, the more we realised what a difficult situation it had been. One of his first extramarital affairs had been with one of his wife's relatives and it started not long after they married. His wife was kept in the dark about her husband's history by members of both her own family and his – several of whom knew only too well the details of Sinclair's past.

During Sinclair's married life there had been frequent periods of time when he'd lived away from the family home. Typically, he worked at his painting jobs through the week in and around Glasgow and then went off at the weekends, regularly staying away until the Monday morning. He was away so often that he didn't find out about the birth of his son, which had occurred on a Saturday, for twenty-four or more hours because he was out and about in Edinburgh.

The pressures mounted and eventually, completely frustrated at Sinclair's inability to assume the role of a normal husband and father, the family split. Time passed and healed some of the problems. Sarah knew of Sinclair's numerous affairs and she had to bear the additional burden of his self-confessed relationships with prostitutes but, despite this, she would allow Sinclair to come back home time and again for the sake of their child.

It was during this rocky period in their marriage that the younger Hamilton moved in with the Sinclairs and his crime career of theft and robbery with Gus began. By then, Sinclair had the caravanette that was to become enormously important to us as it was the vehicle he owned when the World's End murders were committed.

It was also about this time that Sinclair developed an interest in photography. It was thought fairly benign until the day his wife

Sarah found pornographic snaps of Sinclair and a girl taken with a timer device. This caused a huge family row but the photos were burnt and his convoluted explanation for having them was accepted. In hindsight, this new behaviour was significant – especially since it linked Angus Sinclair with a like-minded character, the murdered Eddie Cotogno.

Some people might find it difficult to sympathise with Sarah Sinclair – after all, she knew of some aspects of his criminality and she tolerated it and that may be seen by some as tacit approval. I do not agree with this view. Like many wives and partners of criminals, Sarah found herself sucked into the vortex by an evil and manipulative man. She struggled free and now she deserves to be able to put this awful part of her life behind her. In truth, Sarah Sinclair is another one of Angus Sinclair's victims. She wasn't murdered, raped or even seriously physically attacked but she will bear the scars inflicted by him for the rest of her life.

8

Operation Trinity

In early 2004, as soon as we had DNA linking Angus Sinclair with the World's End case, we began to examine all other murders and disappearances of young women in the late 70s and early 80s very closely – especially those that bore a resemblance in method or modus operandi to the World's End killings. From the start, we were surprised just how many killings there had been in that very narrow time frame. Later, when 'Scothom', the name given to the comprehensive database of homicides of women in Scotland from 1968 to the present, was constructed – a huge and important piece of work done by Strathclyde Police – the picture was even more alarming. We tend to assume that, in the twenty-first century, we are living in the most violent of times. While comparisons are sometimes difficult, the 1970s was no haven of tranquillity either.

After detailed study, however, it appeared that the cases of three women murdered in the Glasgow area – Anna Kenny, Matilda (or Hilda as she was usually called) McAuley and Agnes Cooney – and two in Dundee – Carol Lannen and Elizabeth McCabe – bore close similarities to the World's End ones. Together with Helen and Christine, we had a total of seven victims – young women, from three areas of Scotland, who had all been murdered during the period from August 1977 to February 1980 – and all seven cases remained unsolved. Because of the three distinct areas in the investigation and the three forces involved, the name 'Trinity' was chosen for our combined investigation and, despite the fact

119

that the Dundee cases were quickly eliminated from the inquiry, to subsequently go their own way, the name stuck. I was appointed by the three Chief Constables to be the Officer in Overall Command, tasked with leading the joint effort and ensuring close co-ordination by the different investigation teams from Lothian and Borders Police and Strathclyde Police.

The role of the Officer in Overall Command is a relatively recent innovation which had come about as a result of the inquiry in the aftermath of the Yorkshire Ripper case and had proved successful in several linked cases since. The main criterion for appointment as an Officer in Overall Command was holding the rank of chief officer, having a background in major criminal investigation and having extensive experience in leading large teams. I was fortunate to be qualified for I would have hated to miss the last phase of the World's End investigation. It wasn't, however, the easiest of roles. On the one hand, I was ultimately responsible to the Chief Constables and directly accountable for all aspects of the inquiry. On the other hand, I could not interfere with the individual investigations too much or impede the senior investigating officers in the individual cases. They were highly experienced and senior detectives. Detective Superintendents Ian Thomas and Eddie McCusker, backed by Allan Jones, in Lothian and Borders and Colin Field in Strathclyde were an impressive mix of old heads and young potential. Added to that was the fact that, frankly, they had a lot more recent experience in murder and major crime investigation than I had. In any joint investigation, there will be tensions and competing priorities, with pride and frustration sometimes boiling over but, in the many months we were together, these were always managed and overcome.

I had other advantages. I knew most of the members of the Lothian and Borders team, both police and civilian, personally. Lastly, but importantly, I was given a very good bright young staff officer in Detective Sergeant Stuart Hood and I managed to take my personal assistant Jeanette Shiells with me. Jeanette and I had worked well together for twelve years and she knew my every thought. These details may sound mundane but, in the careful balancing act of the Officer in Overall Command, they were immensely important.

Running a linked investigation, particularly one focused on historic undetected homicides – cold cases – may sound fairly simple but it is not and strict rules and protocols have to be followed if the process is not to become confused and ineffective. For that reason, all police forces in the UK closely follow the 'Cold Case Review Guidance' given by the Association of Chief Police Officers in England and Wales which is based on the long and sometimes bitter experience of murder squad detectives. It may surprise some people that historic undetected homicides are a problem requiring such a complicated response but they are. In the ten years up to 1979, there were over 700 cases of homicide where either no one was charged or the accused was acquitted and that was only in England and Wales.

It is a surprising total but, with new techniques and ever-improving forensic science, I am sure many of these cases will yet be resolved. Now, when police forces embark on a historic re-investigation, it is not only with new forensic tools but with the benefit of the accumulated experience of scores of cases. We now have a better understanding of the value of new forensic techniques, not only in DNA but in how useful fingerprints, hairs and fibres can be to us. The use of lasers, digital imaging and computerised databases all mean that materials recovered from crime scenes and considered worthless may yet have enormous evidential value. But it is not only in new science that advances have been made. The role of expert independent advisers can be of enormous advantage. In our case it was an expert forensic adviser, Professor David Barclay, who was of huge assistance while the advice given by our behavioural psychologist gave us insight into the predicted behaviour of witnesses and suspects, all of which gave us an edge.

121

The World's End Murders

A major element in the World's End case was of course the DNA samples and the hairs and fibres recovered from Helen's clothes. But even this was not straightforward for we had to demonstrate that, over the thirty years they had been in our possession, there had been no opportunity for contamination of the productions. A thirty-year audit trail had to be carried out to prove every movement of materials and the supervision that attended them. It says much for Lester Knibb and his colleagues that this did not defeat us for the records had been meticulously kept.

In linking our inquiries, we always followed the latest guidelines and best practice. In TV dramas and fiction, the officer in charge of murder investigations usually confronts the suspect, dazzling all with his or her deductive skill. In reality, the Officer in Overall Command of a linked investigation must pay more attention to policy files and processes if the investigation is to succeed.

Thankfully, in all of these difficult areas we were helped magnificently by the National Crime and Operations Faculty based at Bramshill in Hampshire. Their knowledge and network of experts provided all the help we needed. The advisory team of experts established to assist us was first class. None of these structures or systems was there to help the detectives in 1977. It would not have occurred to them, even in their wildest dreams, that such methods of working could be possible.

By the summer of 2004, it was clear that we were building a compelling case against Angus Robertson Sinclair for the World's End murders. There was a growing sense of achievement amongst the teams involved in this major, complex and long-running inquiry. We had started the journey with some hope of reaching our goal but, in the early days, there were inevitably doubts that we would be able to reach back through the long passage of time and find the supporting evidence we needed to once and for all allow us to achieve justice in this truly iconic case.

Our trump card was the DNA evidence from the World's End

killings but we also had some circumstantial evidence in the cases of Anna Kenny, Matilda McAuley and Agnes Cooney. We lacked any forensic evidence in these cases, however, and this was crucial. In the end, it was judged by the prosecuting authority in Scotland, the Crown Office, that we simply didn't have a good enough case to prove the matter beyond reasonable doubt and this was a bitter disappointment to all of us. It was especially felt by the Strathclyde team who had done so much to prepare a case against Sinclair for these three murders, based on the little evidence that had survived the passage of time. The lengths they went to in trying to make up the evidence gap were remarkable and their commitment was total.

In the aftermath, much has been made of the lack of forensic evidence in the Glasgow cases. Where were the samples from these cases, were they lost, were they destroyed and, if so, why? We will never know for sure what happened to that forensic evidence but, before the armchair experts and journalists with perfect hindsight begin their critiques, it is worth remembering the state of forensic science back in the 1970s. Forensic work on blood, hair and fibre was already being done but, although the presence of DNA had been proposed by a Swiss doctor in the nineteenth century and Crick and Watson had developed the theory further in 1953, in those days, it was unknown as an investigative tool. Even ten years later, in the late 80s, when I studied at the FBI Academy in Washington, a faculty with limitless resources and cutting-edge forensic facilities, DNA was only beginning to emerge as an aid to detecting crime.

In the late 1970s, the future of DNA was unknown and forensic samples were often tested to destruction during their examination. This may have happened in the Glasgow cases or they may have simply been destroyed, having been deemed as being of no further apparent evidential value. During the investigation in 2004–5, the team from Strathclyde Police had carried out extensive searches for these samples. No stone was left unturned by Detective Superintendent Eddie McCusker and his team but without success. It was a major disappointment to these determined and professional officers, but who knows, the missing forensic samples may yet be discovered, they may yet give up their DNA secrets – stranger things have happened.

The second question was why the senior detectives of the late 70s had not linked the cases back when they were first being investigated and when all the evidence was fresh. The publicity generated by the murders in Edinburgh and Glasgow had been immense. Reading the news clippings of the day, it was clear that there was a public outcry in the truest sense. In addition, some crime reporters were openly linking the cases and claiming that one man was responsible.

On the face of it, the police were not so convinced but formal linking was, in fact, considered as early as 1980. That year, heads of CIDs from Scottish forces with unsolved female murders on their patches held a conference in Perth – a convenient point for them to gather from throughout Scotland. They met to decide if any joint action should be taken by their respective investigations. Should they be linked either publicly or internally in an effort to pool information and speed up detection? In effect, they had to decide whether the crimes were likely to be the work of one man.

No minutes survive from those discussions but the outcome is certain. They decided to continue the inquiries as separate entities with no formal element of linkage. This, I rather fear, was a decision taken out of operational and political pragmatism rather than sound policing instincts.

When seen from the time of Operation Trinity, I believe the judgement of those senior officers was probably influenced by the ghost of the man known in the press as 'Bible John'. There had been a series of three killings of women connected to the Barrowlands dance hall in Glasgow during 1968 and 1969. A single culprit had been created in the minds of journalists and, through them, the public at large. The image of a serial killer had been formed and he had been given the nickname of Bible John because witnesses in one of the murders had spoken of a strange and creepy individual using biblical quotations in his everyday speech at the dance hall on the night of the killing. It was a classic case of the press headline selling the story and, at the time, there was real and widespread public alarm at the thought of Bible John stalking the streets of Glasgow looking for his chance to pounce – a twentieth-century Jack the Ripper.

The true facts of the case are rather different. Whilst many suspects have been in the frame over the years as a potential Bible John, it is entirely possible, even likely, that one man was not responsible for all three killings and there was no Bible John. This, of course, was not a theory favoured by the newspapers that had rather warmed to a homicidal maniac's positive effect on their circulations. The Bible John case has been reopened and reinvestigated on several occasions – a long-dead suspect was even exhumed – but, to this day, there has been no resolution, no real evidence to say that a serial killer ever existed. It may well be that Bible John's victims were in fact murdered by different men in unconnected incidents.

The hysteria of this case would still be fresh in the minds of those senior detectives as they met in Perth and I think they came to the decision not to link the cases until such time as they had over-powering evidence to the contrary, at least in part to prevent another Bible John character being hyped by the press. They didn't need anything that could increase the pressure on them to force their hands or create panic in the community.

What we now know about Angus Sinclair, Gordon Hamilton, the death of Mary Gallagher, the World's End murders and the deaths of Anna Kenny, Hilda McAuley and Agnes Cooney should not be used to condemn the conclusions of the 1980 conference.

The officers in charge then made a pragmatic decision, based on their knowledge at the time. It is easy to be critical in retrospect but we should remember that our discoveries were brought about by the latest scientific techniques which were unknown and inconceivable in 1980. Our unearthing of Angus Sinclair relied on techniques that would have been undreamt of twenty-five years ago.

In our reviews of the cases being re-examined by Operation Trinity, it was clear that Sinclair had, at no time, featured contemporaneously in any of the earlier Glasgow killings or the World's End case and nor was any reason uncovered to suggest that he should have. By that I mean we did not find any statement or piece of evidence that linked him directly or indirectly to the murders.

In cold case investigations, it is every detective's nightmare that the culprit's identity appeared in the early investigation system – that he or she was there all the time and the clues were missed. Finding that a killer was actually questioned but had managed to deceive the interviewers and was therefore eliminated from an investigation is something everyone dreads. Most police officers who have worked on long-running inquiries will know what I mean. As an investigation drags on without a solution, doubts start to creep in. There is an old maxim in murder inquiries that says that the solution usually lies in the first five hundred statements – in other words, with those who are most closely connected to the case. Given that murder is usually domestic or by the hand of an associate, this is often true so, in the dark of the night, you can begin to doubt, to question. Did I miss something? Has he got past me?

Over the years, I've kept in contact with a number of retired officers who had worked on the World's End inquiry. As Operation Trinity began, they knew we had a culprit in our sights but they weren't really interested in the name. They only had one question –

had he appeared in the system of earlier investigations? When I was able to tell them that he hadn't, the relief on their faces was apparent. After all those years, their professional pride was still such that they didn't want to be the ones who had slipped up.

Returning to the present, despite the new science, we still had challenges in the World's End case for we had yet to prove the association between Sinclair and Hamilton as well as establish their links to the World's End pub and East Lothian.

The other priorities in investigating all five of the murders were common to all the cases. We had to prove the suspect's knowledge of both the abduction and disposal sites and also show there had been access to vehicles that could have been used for the disposals. In addition, we would have to reinterview all the significant witnesses who were still alive and traceable and, finally, we had to interview our suspect.

This last objective, the questioning of Sinclair, would be a major exercise in itself, requiring detailed planning and careful execution. That would come at the end of the plans I have outlined and it would be made more difficult by the fact that Sinclair was already a prisoner and, as such, entitled to all the protection of a man who was not at liberty and therefore not best able to defend himself. You can argue the rights and wrongs of this but the facts remain – the rules and regulations, the laws, and the strict codes of practice established to protect the innocent also unfortunately protect the guilty.

In 2004, we felt that, overall, the five murders we were dealing with bore such striking similarities that, when viewed as a whole against a background of the circumstances of other unsolved murders of women in Scotland, they were unique. Often a killer will leave some telltale sign, a signature that is theirs alone, or perhaps follow a similar pattern of criminal behaviour. This is simply a factor of human behaviour. We all, knowingly and unknowingly, develop patterns of behaviour, some learned in childhood, some adopted and adapted as we learn from life's experience. It's often said that the best way to predict an individual's future behaviour is to explore their past. This is as true of criminal behaviour as of any other. In these cases, the points of comparison between each murder were significant and bear examination.

Each victim – Helen Scott, Christine Eadie, Anna Kenny, Matilda McAuley and Agnes Cooney – was abducted within an hour either way of midnight on a Friday or Saturday during the second half of 1977. Each victim had been socialising and had been drinking sufficiently for their guard to be lowered. Each victim was taken without a single witness seeing the moment of abduction – a clear sign of careful planning and organisation, especially as they occurred in areas with lots of people going about on busy weekend nights.

Each body was disposed of in a similar way. They were all dumped near quiet roads, out of sight of any nearby highway. This allowed the person getting rid of the body to be certain they would not be seen and they were then able to make a speedy escape. Even the deposition site of Christine Eadie, near the coast road from Edinburgh to East Lothian, had good sight lines in the hours of darkness to ensure the disposal of the body would not be seen by a passing car. Each girl was tied up – usually both hands and feet but in one case it was just her feet – and most of the ligatures were made using items of their own clothing.

The similarities go on but, as the cases of Anna, Matilda and Agnes remain open, it would be wrong to go into any more detail here or to reveal details of the evidence we gathered. It is just possible that a prosecution may yet be brought in these cases. Suffice to say that, from our standpoint, it all looked pretty compelling – these crimes looked to have been committed by the same person but, to prove it, we needed to place these cases in context and compare them with all the other murders of women in Scotland over the period to test their uniqueness.

We were dealing with five murders in six months. Through DNA evidence, we knew, beyond any doubt, that Sinclair was involved in two of them. We also had assorted other crimes woven in between the weekend murders that Sinclair was also suspected of. To prove just how out of the ordinary these murder cases were, Operation Trinity embarked on the biggest survey of murders of women in Scotland ever undertaken.

It was all very well to look at the circumstances and say that, superficially, there are strong links between the five murders and conclude they are the work of the same killer. However, we had to show, beyond all reasonable doubt, that these killings were unique. In the end, we failed but, in the process, a hugely important database had been developed. It was useful for both our own research and future investigations.

It was not only essential to look at the unsolved murders of women but also to examine all unlawful killings of females to try to show just how singular the five murders were. We needed to look in some detail at every single murder of a female in Scotland and, from the details of these killings, compile a database. As ever with the Police Service, the enterprise needed a name and so 'Operation Scothom' came into being. As the database was being designed and built up, the Trinity management team were only too aware of how vital the task facing us was. The decision was taken to make the starting point of our examination some years before Sinclair came on the scene and take it right up to the time for which latest records were available. So four decades of death were studied in exhaustive depth between the years 1968 and 2003. There was only one rule for membership of this wretched club – the person needed to have been female, dead and have her had death attributed to murder.

As with any enterprise of this nature, it was crucially important to go into it with a highly systematic approach to ensure the results that came out of the other end were true reflections of the facts. Furthermore, it was imperative for the operation to be geared in such a way that all aspects of every murder could be identified and compared with every other killing. We could not fall victims to self-delusion or go looking for the result we wanted to make the pieces fit. Our finished product would have to stand scrutiny for we could be sure that, if the results of this work were ever to be put before a jury, it was extremely likely that they would be vigorously challenged. The world, and particularly the legal profession, is amply populated by those whose mission is to find fault so whatever we did had to be substantial enough to withstand all scrutiny.

In this piece of work this was particularly true. As with every aspect of any criminal investigation, we needed to be constantly aware that, one day, a defence lawyer would be going through our work with an eye to discovering inconsistencies, omissions or prejudice that undermined the conclusions. One flaw or one error would render the exercise worthless. We sometimes forget that the defence advocate or solicitor in a criminal case is only responsible for preparing and delivering the best possible case for the defendant. They are not concerned with justice.

Many prominent defence lawyers have made the discovery of procedural irregularities, human errors or simple mistakes their stock-in-trade. We had to make sure our database was bulletproof. The man given the task to lead this effort was the able and highly experienced Detective Inspector Derek Robertson of Strathclyde Police. He would need all his skill in the coming months.

Much of this work was carried out by officers from the eight police forces of Scotland who were not connected to our investigation. It was essential that the operation was kept as straightforward as possible so we devised a form to be completed for every murder that would ensure each case was looked at in a similar way and the details logged into the computer in exactly the same way so that accurate comparisons could be made.

It surprised most of us that, during this period of time, a total of 1,038 women were murdered in Scotland. This figure does not include those who died aboard Pan Am Flight 103 over Lockerbie on 21 December 1988.

The task was another major undertaking for the whole of the Scottish Police Service in this inquiry and individual officers in each of the eight areas were responsible for co-ordinating their force's contribution to the database. It sounds easy but in fact it was a complex job to trace and examine all the files and records, some of which were nearly forty years old.

More than any other crime, murder is the one that has the biggest effect on the community where it happens. Each case, by definition the illegal taking of life, is a devastating blow for those most closely connected to it. Whilst murder rightly holds this place as the most abhorrent of crimes, it is fair to say that the different categories have vastly different impacts. The murder of a child stays in the public's mind for a long time whereas the murder of a criminal or a vagrant living rough on the streets rather less so. I highlight this only to demonstrate just how difficult it is to uncover details of every one of those one thousand plus murders stretching back so far in time. We were not just looking at unsolved killings but at all the murders reported in Scotland. The wide time parameters of the exercise meant that many of the cases we were examining had been investigated, prosecuted, the case closed and the perpetrator already freed from jail or in some cases dead. Details of many of these murders were hard to track down. To be a worthwhile tool in the prosecution of Sinclair, however, the database had to be a complete examination of every case so each one had to be traced and eventually they all were. The Scothom database was a hugely important piece of work but, like many important things in life, it was difficult to achieve. It was also to throw up a problem that we had not expected.

Traceability and accountability were obviously vital for this operation. The exercise was based in Cathcart police station in Glasgow to where the responsible officers in each of Scotland's police forces reported. They were briefed to examine these records in minute detail and to extract all the significant factors surrounding each case. They would only have been aware in the most general terms of the importance of their endeavours but we went to great lengths to ensure they all realised just how crucial the task in hand was. There could be no room for error, corner-cutting or lack of attention to detail.

The database that was constructed as a result of this painstaking work would, we believed, be of considerable use to police forces in the future. Researchers and criminologists would also be able to consult the findings for academic purposes.

In addition to this research, the pathologists connected to the Scottish police forces went through a similar operation under the guidance of two of the country's senior practitioners from the University of Glasgow. The university lab had detailed knowledge of our case and had already been of immense help.

All the Operation Trinity murders we were examining bore a similar signature in the method of killing and how the bodies were left but the Scothom database threw up something else. It showed there was the possibility of a sixth killing fitting the pattern. Once a murder is 'solved', it tends to slip from the collective memory of the criminal justice system and the press – file closed. So it was no surprise that the name of Frances Barker meant little to us when we were first told about the striking similarities between her killing and the five murders being examined by us. The only difference was that, in the Barker case, a culprit had been identified, prosecuted and imprisoned for life.

Apart from the murder of Frances Barker and the other five murders, the results from Scothom were exactly what we had expected them to be. As has already been noted, all our victims had been gagged with an item of their own clothing. In the thirty-seven-year period we examined, only three other female murder victims had been gagged but none of them with items of clothing and all three killings had taken place inside buildings of one sort or another. In short, apart from the gag, they bore no similarities to our five cases, rendering the link so tenuous as to be irrelevant.

So what did the murder of Frances Barker mean to our inquiry? Firstly, the circumstances of her death and body disposal were so similar to those of the World's End murders that her name was immediately added to the list of deaths we were interested in. However, we had to begin a new inquiry into her murder to discover which of four possibilities had come about. I say four because, whatever had happened in this case, that was the sum of the different potential circumstances that had occurred. To spell it out, there was a limited number of options as to what had happened:

a) Frances Barker had been murdered by Sinclair and there had been a miscarriage of justice;
b) Frances Barker had been murdered by Sinclair acting together with the man already convicted of the crime;
c) Sinclair had been schooled in murder by the man convicted of Frances Barker's death;
d) the man convicted of Frances Barker's murder happened to use the same MO as Sinclair.

It was clear from the very first time the case came to the attention of senior officers that, no matter which of these four possibilities had occurred, the case of Frances Barker was going to be problematic for our inquiry. In those early days of our knowing of this murder, I think we all rather hoped option b) or c) would present itself as the eventual outcome. It would be some time before a conclusion could be reached though and a very thorough, painstaking investigation was undertaken.

The date of Frances Barker's death, 11 June 1977, would have made her the first victim of the six months of murder. She was thirty-seven and lived alone in a flat in the Maryhill district of

Glasgow, having moved out of the family home in the city centre. Frances had worked for a baker in Glasgow for more than four years prior to her death and the company was, in fact, the landlord of her new flat.

The night she met her death she had, like all the other victims, been out socialising and had had a fair amount to drink. I think it would be fair to say that, by the time her sister and other family members she had been with that night helped her into a taxi to go home, she was a little worse for wear.

The taxi driver who dropped her off that night remembered clearly watching his fare as she made a somewhat precarious way towards the door of her close, in Glasgow's Maryhill Road. The cabbie did not actually see Frances go into the close because it was a busy Glasgow Friday night and another fare climbed aboard the taxi as soon as Frances got out and the taxi was off.

After her murder the police discovered that it was unlikely she would have been able to gain entry to the close that night. She had mistakenly taken the wrong coat from the pub where they had been earlier that night and her house keys had been left in her own coat in that pub.

Her colleagues at the bakery were no doubt concerned when Frances didn't appear for work the following Monday and, indeed, for the rest of that week but their concern did not cause them to take any action until the Friday – a full week since they had last seen her. They contacted Frances's parents and, later that day, bakery workers and Frances's brother Tom went to the flat in Maryhill Road and forced their way in. There was no trace of her and no sign of a disturbance or of anything being out of place.

A full sixteen days later, a man working on his family's farm near Glenboig in Lanarkshire found the badly decomposed remains of a woman lying in a copse next to a farm road. He immediately ran home to get his father and the pair returned a short time later to confirm what the young man had feared – that he had found a body. The police were called and, along with the police surgeon, a careful examination of the scene was made. In what was to become a depressingly familiar pattern over the next few months of 1977, the victim was found to be bound hand and foot, her legs tied together with part of her tights, her arms restrained by her scarf. Her underwear had been used as a gag and this was kept in place by the rest of her tights. Branches and leaves had been scattered over the body to hide it. The area where the body was dumped was similar to the other disposal sites – hidden from view. It was June and the concealment had been made easier by the rich foliage on surrounding trees and bushes.

The post-mortem carried out at the time suggested that Frances had been strangled with some force. There was no evidence of sexual assault but the body was badly decomposed.

An extensive police inquiry over a period of some weeks failed to find a single witness who had seen Frances after she left the taxi in the early hours of Saturday morning. She had seemingly vanished off the face of the earth.

Reading the old files and cuttings, it seemed that detectives got an early break in the investigations and a man was arrested and subsequently convicted. At the time of writing, there are active legal proceedings concerning this man so I can't go into details about his identity.

Suffice to say that Maryhill, the area where Frances Barker went missing, was Sinclair's home territory. He was brought up on the edge of the district and his mother still lived there at the time of the Barker killing. Our background inquiries into Sinclair suggested that, on the night of Frances's abduction, Sinclair was probably staying with his mother in Maryhill Road as he was going through one of his frequent separations from Sarah.

The site where the body was found would also have been well known to Sinclair – it was near to the place where a friend used to repair Sinclair's cars. To prove the connection, we had interviewed some other associates of Sinclair and they told us that, about the time of the killing, he had been talking about buying and renovating a rundown cottage close to where Frances's body was found. These two strands of information made it abundantly clear that he had a detailed knowledge of the area.

When Frances Barker disappeared, Sinclair was driving a Toyota Carina car but, just a few days later, he got rid of it and bought the Toyota caravanette that was to be his weekend recreation vehicle. At the time of the World's End killings, he still owned the caravanette and, in all likelihood, he used it to transport Helen Scott and Christine Eadie to East Lothian on what was to be their last journey.

9

The Death of Anna Kenny

The lack of forensic evidence in the Glasgow cases was a huge obstacle from the start. It was clear that, to stand any chance of a successful prosecution, we had to go to extraordinary lengths to establish connections between Sinclair and the scenes of crimes, the places where the women were last seen and where the bodies were found. From the original statements, we had to trace possible sightings of Sinclair or vehicles he may have driven at the time. In addition, we had to trawl through and meticulously record all the murders of women in Scotland over a near forty-year period to try to demonstrate the unique similarities of the five crimes.

Even with all this done to the very best of our abilities, we knew that the chances were slim. The burden of proof in the criminal court – beyond all reasonable doubt – is a tough standard, as it should be. In the end, Angus Sinclair only stood trial for the World's End murders of Helen Scott and Christine Eadie.

The solution to the 1978 case of Mary Gallagher was brought about through an incorrect tip-off from a member of the public which was to lead to the re-examination of the evidence which, in turn, allowed Glasgow detectives to find an exact DNA match with Sinclair. The three other cases linked to Sinclair by the press in the aftermath of that conviction were not going to be so straight-forward. Samples and productions from the crime scenes in the murders of the three women had, unfortunately, not survived the passage of time.

It is important to state clearly here the basis for including the account of these three unsolved murders in the narrative of the World's End case. Angus Sinclair has not been charged in connection with the deaths of Anna Kenny, Matilda McAuley and Agnes Cooney. These crimes remain unsolved and neither I nor the team who worked with me on Operation Trinity would wish to jeopardise any future prosecution. The fact is, however, that we did reopen these cases and the team from Strathclyde Police led by Detective Superintendent Eddie McCusker thoroughly re-investigated them. The description of this process is relevant to this story but it is important to repeat that no one has been charged with these crimes and that no facts or evidence, not already in the public domain, will be discussed here.

I will make no further comment on the guilt or innocence of anyone in these cases – readers must judge for themselves.

From the start, the reinvestigation of the three cases, bound together by a raft of similarities, came up against a considerable obstacle – the lack of hard evidence.

Strathclyde officers had already reviewed the evidence they had in the cases of Anna Kenny, Matilda McAuley and Agnes Cooney and, shortly after Sinclair's 2001 conviction for the Gallagher murder, they concluded that they could not present a prima facie case against anyone. Without the kind of forensic evidence that had been crucial in the Gallagher conviction, it would only have been possible to present a circumstantial case. There was a powerful set of circumstances but not powerful enough to put to a jury. So it was that Operation Trinity presented probably the last best chance of discovering exactly what happened to the three women and identifying the man, or men, responsible. To overcome the absence of forensic evidence, we were going to have to take a whole new approach to the cases which had already been subjected to extensive investigation and reinvestigation.

It is important to clarify one thing at this point. The 1970s investigations of these three cases were the best they could have been, given the time in which they occurred and the relatively primitive forensic science of the day. Each case was led by officers who were the foremost of their peers and our revisiting of the files turned up no glaring errors or omissions that left them unsolved for so long. These officers did the very best they could with what they had at the time.

The way forward was to establish all possible links and similarities between the three murders and then see whether they matched the circumstances of the World's End case. Then, with analysis of the minute detail of every aspect of all the cases, we would try to establish evidential links between them all, to bind them together.

The chilling fact behind this endeavour was the knowledge that, if we could establish these links and prove that one man or a group of men were responsible for all the murders, it would mean that, in seven months in 1977, he or they had been on a sex killing spree unparalleled in British criminal history. If Sinclair was involved, these crimes would have been committed while, to the outside world, he was a hard-working painter and decorator, living with his wife and five-year-old son.

By this time in our inquiries, we were already in close consultation with the Crown Office in Edinburgh – the prosecuting authority for Scotland. The relationship between the police in Scotland, the investigators, and the Crown Office is an interesting one. All prosecutions in Scotland, with the exception of a tiny number of private prosecutions, are raised in the name of the Lord Advocate and his or her officers, the procurators fiscal. The fiscals prosecute in the lower courts while counsel known as advocates-depute prosecute in the higher courts. The relationship between the Crown Office, the Lord Advocate and his or her officers and the police is seen as odd and anachronistic by some observers. In fact, it is straightforward and seasoned over hundreds of years so that everyone knows their roles and responsibilities. It is sometimes seen as too close and cosy and others, from a different perspective, may claim it is an antagonistic relationship, with police and prosecutors appearing to be working to different agendas. In my experience, it is neither of these. The Crown Office rightly preserves its independence and its discretion over whether to prosecute. In a system of independent prosecution, this is the way of the world and, although there are sometimes differences of opinion, the lines of demarcation are clear.

The niceties of the prosecution system were not, however, in the forefront of our minds as we began to examine the three cases. The Strathclyde team was facing the huge task of unpacking three separate thirty-year-old murder investigations – and sometimes it was quite literally a matter of unpacking as dozens of boxes of old files had to be opened and their contents meticulously examined. These cases had, of course, all been reviewed before but there was no alternative to starting again – going back to the beginning and working slowly through all the evidence, applying the latest investigative techniques. The scale of the task was daunting but Eddie McCusker and his team set about it in a scrupulous and determined manner.

The case of the first of these victims to be killed, Anna Kenny from Glasgow, was first to be examined and it produced one of the most bizarre twists of any murder investigation I have ever been involved in.

Anna was just twenty when she met her death. She'd been on a night out with her best friend, Wilma Sutherland. It was just another ordinary tale of ordinary girls going about their everyday lives. Anna and Wilma seemed to do everything together. They had just started temporary but well-paid jobs on a brewery bottling line in Port Dundas in Glasgow. Previously they had worked together at a number of different jobs in and around Glasgow and had once left the city for work, again together, for jobs at the Butlin's holiday camp in Filey, North Yorkshire.

So it was against this background of close friendship that they had arranged to meet up in the High Street of Glasgow, opposite the city's Royal Infirmary, to go out and spend their first wages from the new jobs at the bottling plant. Although they were being paid more than they earned in previous jobs, they didn't have a lot of cash that Friday night, 5 August 1977, but were determined to make the best of it.

A new pub called the Hurdy Gurdy had opened in the Townhead area of Glasgow. It was just the latest thing and the place to be seen for girls of Wilma and Anna's age and so that was where they headed for. After a couple of wrong turnings along the way, the pair eventually arrived at the Hurdy Gurdy and so began just another Friday night. They stayed in the bar for the entire evening drinking a potent mixture of vodka and beer and chatting to various friends who passed through the pub at different stages of the evening. Towards the end of the night, they fell into the company of two young men who I will just call Willie and Joe. Willie had gone to the bar in the expectation of meeting up with a friend who, in the event, didn't show up. He knew Joe and was happy to join him and the two girls, Wilma and Anna. It was a decision that would cause him a lot of heartache and trouble over the next few years. Joe was anxious to walk Wilma home but feared she wouldn't go with him if it meant leaving Anna on her own. So it was that Wilma and Joe and Willie and Anna left the bar that night as couples.

Wilma stayed chatting and kissing Joe in a doorway for a while, having first seen that her by-now tipsy friend Anna was allright with Willie. Willie said that he and Anna kissed for a while but she made it clear that was it and she was going to go home. Willie was married with a newborn child at home and so he too thought it best

141

to call it a night and head off as well. When he left her, Anna appeared to be trying to flag down a taxi. He had no way of knowing it but, when Willie caught that fleeting image of Anna, he was the last person known to see her alive.

Just as in the cases of the Edinburgh girls Helen and Christine, no abduction was seen, nothing happened on the night of Anna's disappearance to raise the alarm and it was not until the following morning when Wilma went round to her friend's house that Anna was found to be missing. Later that Saturday afternoon, Wilma, by now distraught with worry, alerted Anna's family and she was reported missing. There was no quick solution to this mystery and the longer Anna was missing the more concerned the police and her family became. That said, there was still nothing to suggest for certain that her disappearance was sinister but the longer it went on, the more all concerned feared the worst.

The response of the police to reports of a missing person in the first twelve to twenty-four hours is crucial. I will discuss this further but it's very often difficult to get it right. Every weekend across the country dozens of mainly young people go missing for a day or a night. Whether it's a party that lasts overnight, a new friendship or a last-minute decision to take a trip, in the vast majority of cases, the missing person turns up safe and well.

As time went by, however, experience and instinct would suggest to the police that something untoward must have happened to the missing girl and the intensity of the investigation into the mystery that they began made it clear to us that Anna's continued disappearance was taken very seriously.

This brings me back to the vexed question of missing persons, a subject which had concerned me for much of my police service. It is quite staggering just how many people go missing each year. It's reckoned that, annually, 210,000 people are reported missing in the UK. Two thirds of them are young people and, of course, the vast majority are found or return home – usually within a few days. But a significant number are not traced, do not return home and are never heard of again. They simply disappear. I believe that, throughout the UK, we have not dealt with this problem seriously or systematically enough. It's time for a re-examination of the way missing person cases are treated and I'll tell you why.

Very early on in any missing person inquiry, the police service will make a value judgement on the case and decide the level of resource that is to be allocated. Let me illustrate this with extreme examples. If a child of tender years vanishes, within minutes of the report to police, a major operation swings into place. In fact, after the child abductions and murders by Robert Black, the van driver convicted of three such killings in the 1980s, the importance of a fast response was apparent and detailed plans were drawn up by all police forces as to how to respond to such cases. A strict protocol – 'Operation Child Watch' – was developed.

Now, if abduction is even suspected, within minutes of the police being alerted, major roads are under surveillance both by officers on the spot in cars and through all the technical means to hand. At the other extreme is the disappearance of a troublesome young person, with a history of running away, who is deemed old enough to look after themselves. In that case, a very different scenario unfolds. If the person is over sixteen, the age when they are entitled to go off somewhere without letting others know, then it's likely that very little will be done immediately to trace them unless there is compelling evidence that there are suspicious circumstances. With this approach, much valuable time can be lost. If a week or so passes before a non-suspicious missing person inquiry is elevated and prioritised, then the most important time in any investigation is lost. And it's not just time that's lost. Delays mean that forensic opportunities, the recall of witnesses and – most important of all – the impetus are all gone.

At any given time, there are up to 150 cases throughout the

UK where human remains have been found and lie unidentified. Charities do good work in trying to identify them and trace relatives but many are eventually cremated or buried in unmarked graves – the bleak testimony to lives that have simply fallen between the cracks of an inadequate system.

It can be difficult for the police for other reasons because there are a significant number of people who, for one reason or another, want to vanish. It may be personal, financial or family reasons that drive someone to disappear but, unless a crime has been committed, there is no reason for the police to be overly involved especially if it seems the individual just wanted to drop out of view. It is sometimes simply the case that the person's life has just become too much for them and they feel a fresh start, unburdened by the baggage of their former existence, is the only way forward. And that's fair enough – after all, in missing person's inquiries, like all other police activities, the resources to deal with all the problems presenting themselves to the force are finite and priorities need to be established. However, that does not get away from the fact that we often have no idea what the real circumstances of a missing person are and it is a simple fact that persistent runaways tend to mix with some of the less desirable people on the fringes of society who may well see the chance to commit crime with little fear of detection. You need only look at how long Fred and Rose West went about their business of abduction and murder without being discovered to see what I mean.

It is certain that, in the early days of the missing person's inquiry into Anna's disappearance, some suspicion would have fallen on the boy Willie – not least because of the fact that, in the light of his personal circumstances, he at first denied being with Anna in the minutes before she vanished. Fortunately for him, it was clear from the files on the original investigation that detectives eventually eliminated him from their inquiries and determined that he had nothing to do with her disappearance, not least because his walk home that night had luckily been punctuated with meetings with friends who, when traced, could vouch for his movements. His alibi was complete though his activities that night may well have been the source of considerable domestic stress.

The priority given to this missing person's inquiry was such that it was clearly feared, from early on in the investigation, that some terrible fate had befallen Anna. The difficulty of detecting the random killer is perfectly illustrated here. Whoever took Anna as she looked for a taxi that night was not seen and extensive inquiries and appeals for help from the public produced no leads. There was no car being driven in a suspicious manner; there were no unexplained sightings of rowing couples; no one saw a struggle; and there was no body, no scene of crime, no weapon, no forensics, no witnesses. Anna had simply vanished.

We had by this time tracked down and finally identified Gordon Hamilton as the man who had left the main samples of DNA at the World's End scenes of crime. Long dead, his was the DNA that we had been trying to identify for years and that we had eventually identified by his familial links with the Hamilton family, Angus Sinclair's in-laws.

As I've already said, Wilma Sutherland had been with Anna in the Hurdy Gurdy on the night she disappeared. When she realised Anna hadn't been home after she'd last seen her in the company of the man she'd left the pub with, Wilma had searched in vain for her best friend. She had raised the alarm and reported Anna as a missing person and, along with family members, had been in the forefront of the hunt for Anna. So imagine our surprise when we discovered that Wilma had married Gordon Hamilton just over a year after Anna's disappearance.

They had begun a relationship after meeting one night in the self-same Hurdy Gurdy bar. They had met after Anna vanished but before her body was found many months later in remote Kintyre.

It may never be known what role, if any, Gordon Hamilton

played in Anna's disappearance but his connection with the Hurdy Gurdy and Anna's friend, albeit after her disappearance, gave us a tantalising puzzle to consider. Not least was the question about Sinclair's modus operandi. We now knew he had been with Gordon Hamilton at the scene of the World's End murders yet, as far as we were aware, his other sexual crimes were committed alone. We knew from witnesses that he had certainly been alone in the murder of Mary Gallagher. The exception seemed to be the Edinburgh killings – the difference there of course being the fact that there were two victims.

However, one thing was certain – Wilma Sutherland had, quite unwittingly, married one of the men at the centre of the World's End case. This strange twist became even more bizarre as we uncovered further details. Wilma only went back to the Hurdy Gurdy bar twice after Anna's disappearance and, on one of those occasions, she had met Gordon Hamilton and fallen into conversation with him. It was just before Christmas 1977 and they soon began going out with each other. They got married in October 1978 and some six months later, on 23 April 1979, Anna's remains were found in a shallow grave in a remote and beautiful area of Argyll at the start of the Kintyre peninsula. Only her skeleton remained but she had been bound just like Christine Eadie in the World's End case. The long period of burial had removed the chances of finding significant forensic evidence.

Was Gordon Hamilton involved in the murder of Anna Kenny? If he was not, did he know who was? Was his meeting and subsequent marriage to Wilma Sutherland sheer coincidence? These are three questions I would dearly like to know the answers to. If he was not involved in the killing and did not know who was involved in Anna's death, then the coincidence of his meeting and marrying Anna's best friend is truly remarkable.

For Wilma, it was clear that her marriage to Gordon Hamilton had been a bad move almost from the start. On looking back, she admitted to us that she was simply at a loss to say why she had entered into this union – her only possible explanation was that the pain and puzzlement of Anna's disappearance had left her disorientated and vulnerable. Her life with Gordon was difficult to say the very least. He drank heavily, he was violent towards her and he had extramarital affairs.

He was with her the day police came to their house to tell her that they suspected Anna's body had been found on the west coast some couple of hours' drive from Glasgow. Hamilton even accompanied his wife on visits to Anna's distraught parents. Could a murderer be so detached, so callous, as to sit offering comfort to his victim's family and her best friend, the woman he had made his wife?

During their short marriage, Wilma got to know various members of Hamilton's large family. Her impression of the Hamiltons would have been the same as that of everyone else. Even to the casual observer, they were what might at best be described for the large part as a troubled family.

Gordon's role in the World's End murders had been established by the presence of his DNA and by excluding the other Hamiltons through comparing their profiles with the forensic sample. The scientists told us that DNA testing had shown it was a Hamilton sibling but not one of the living ones – so it had to be the dead one. However, much more proof would be needed to finally confirm Gordon Hamilton's role in Helen and Christine's murders. The first step would be to find a sample of DNA that we could prove beyond doubt came from him. He had only been dead a few years but as I have already described this was still not an easy job.

The search for details of Gordon Hamilton was complicated by the fact that most of Gordon's male siblings were suffering from mental health or drink problems or both. Some of them were unaware of exactly how many brothers or sisters they had and there wasn't one member of this family group, male or female, who had kept in touch with all the others. The only member of this sorry group who stands out as different from the rest of the family is Sarah, who was actually christened Sadie. Both before and since her marriage to Angus Sinclair, she struggled to make something of her life and succeeded in doing so as she pursued a long and valued career in nursing.

Family members appeared to have been aware of certain dark events in the past of Angus Sinclair, the young man who married their sister Sarah, but none was sure of the exact nature of the problem. As we interviewed them almost thirty years later with in some cases large parts of recall of their lives lost, some of the family thought Sinclair had spent time in jail for molesting children. No one was sure of the precise nature of his crime that was of course the sexually motivated murder of Catherine Reehill.

Of the males, the most lucid was one of the older brothers. He was as helpful as he could be considering he had lost touch with some of his brothers and sisters. Importantly, he was happy to supply us with a swab to allow his DNA to be examined. The test proved conclusively that he was not Sinclair's accomplice in the World's End.

He spoke of Gordon as someone who he did not get on with because he didn't like his brother's annoyingly condescending attitude. Gordon seemed to think he was rather better than the rest of his nine brothers and sisters and looked down his nose at them. Ian was able to confirm that Gordon was dead. He had been living with a woman in Glasgow and it was thought they had had a son. He had, however, no recollection of ever seeing either the wife or supposed son despite having been in fairly regular contact with Gordon prior to his death in 1996.

It is normal police practice in an interview like the one we were conducting with this man not to give precise reasons behind our questions for fear of silencing the witness, clouding answers or leading a witness in a particular direction. Officers listened to him quietly, gently probing as he tried his best to search his memory and recall details of his five brothers and four sisters. He was of course rather inquisitive as to what lay behind our visit. However, as soon as it became obvious to him that we were particularly interested in Sarah, he got the connection straightaway and said, 'It's about that animal she got in tow with, isn't it?'

On having his suspicions confirmed, Sarah's brother told us how he hadn't cared for Sinclair from the very first moment he had met him. His sister had brought her then new boyfriend to their parents' home in Tummel Street in Glasgow and, whilst he couldn't put his finger on quite why, Sarah's brother vividly remembered taking an instant and deep dislike to Sinclair – to the extent that, on future visits by Sinclair, if he was at home, he would immediately get up and walk out rather than spend time in what he regarded as his home with this new but disagreeable man in Sarah's life.

This particular brother was serving a term of imprisonment in Glasgow when Sinclair was arrested in 1980 for the series of rapes and indecencies against children, the crimes for which he was eventually to receive his first life sentence. He told us that the news of the arrest and sentence of such a serious offender was the talk of Glasgow's Barlinnie Prison with, no doubt, various practitioners of jail justice vowing to take revenge against Sinclair if they ever got the chance. For understandable reasons, he thought it best not to mention the object of all this interest was, in fact, his brother-in-law.

My years of experience in criminal investigations have taught me that speculating on what might have been is usually a fruitless pastime. At best, it can distract you from the more important task of establishing the facts. At worst, it can mislead and distort the course of an investigation. However, I must confess the motivation behind Gordon Hamilton's marriage to Wilma was the source of much theorising and speculation based on what had to be a simple choice. The marriage was the strangest coincidence ever, the act of a man callous in the extreme or, more tantalisingly, the act of a man drawn back to the scene of the crime, compelled to stay close, stay in control to the extent that he sought a relationship with the person closest to the victim – we will never know.

It is difficult to imagine the tensions that must exist in the relationship between partners in such a crime as the World's End murders. Did it lead to a lifelong bond between Gordon Hamilton and Sinclair? Did they become confidants, bonded together by their shared experience, or was there distrust and tension? In serious crimes where there are a number of culprits, the danger is always that one will talk, to gain some advantage or through fear, and betray the secret. Angus Sinclair's history made him a good bet to keep quiet but Gordon Hamilton must have represented a threat to Sinclair's security. Had he known about his brother-in-law's lifestyle, his heavy drinking and his decline during the 80s, Sinclair must have been concerned about the possibility of Gordon letting something slip. But, by this time, he was in prison and, if he was aware of Gordon's condition, there was nothing he could have done to intervene or influence things.

If Sinclair heard about Gordon's death, he must have breathed a sigh of relief. With the only man who could incriminate him for the World's End murders dead, his secret was safe . . . or so he thought.

Gordon Hamilton was beyond our reach but what we know of him leaves intriguing questions. Could it really be that Gordon Hamilton was a one-off offender? Was a crime of such savagery as the World's End murders his first serious offence and did he then just go back to his everyday life? Could it be that there was a master–servant relationship between the two men in which Gordon Hamilton was the subservient partner? This final possibility seems likely for it is clear that, throughout his adult life, no one told Angus Sinclair what to do. However, unless new evidence not available to our inquiry comes to light, these questions will have to remain unanswered.

Clues though were to be found in what the second youngest Hamilton brother was able to tell us. Unlike his older brother, he had a fairly good relationship with Angus Sinclair. Sinclair had managed to get him a job with one of the painting firms he worked for following his release after his first long prison sentence for the Reehill killing. Then Sinclair gave the boy a second job, so to speak – an apprenticeship as a junior partner in his violent crime enterprises.

The young Hamilton moved into the home where Angus and Sarah were living in Queenslie in the tough east end of Glasgow. He and Sinclair worked away from home from time to time and their friendship was not diminished even after he learned from others of Sinclair's conviction for killing a child. The younger man was of the view that everyone deserved a second chance in life and, anyway, it was a long time ago.

He told officers frankly how he and Sinclair would often return at night to the business premises where they had been painting during the day to steal. This progressed to till snatches at various shops in and around Glasgow. The younger Hamilton admitted that he worried about the extreme violence Sinclair used in these raids. He remembered vividly the day Sinclair mercilessly beat a young girl who had got in his way with a hammer and then, shortly after- wards, he vented his rage at his apprentice for not joining in the cruel attack.

This member of the Hamilton family also told us that Sinclair had been involved extensively with prostitutes in the Glasgow area and on occasions had used information gleaned from them to select other criminal targets. We were able to verify his accounts of his activities with Sinclair as some of the old crime records still existed. Nobody would ever be prosecuted for these crimes – the passage of time was too great – but they were valuable nonetheless. They served to establish, beyond doubt, the character and nature of Angus Sinclair as a violent, ruthless, cool-headed man whose offences were premeditated. The traits he displayed in his crimes of violence were also present in his crimes against young girls and in the murders he committed.

As we progressed and began to piece together the jigsaw of Angus Sinclair's life and criminal career, we started to focus on his means of transport. We knew he had to have the use of a vehicle during the World's End abductions and murders and it had to be big enough to hold four people. Also, Sinclair was travelling fair distances throughout the country so he would need something reliable. As in all serious criminal investigations, we had numerous sightings of vehicles at or near the various crime scenes. Many were vague but some were not and, as it turned out, the cars Angus Sinclair drove in the late 70s were to play a major part in the jigsaw.

We were particularly interested in finding out details of a white caravanette we knew Sinclair had owned in the late 70s at the time of Anna Kenny's disappearance. One such vehicle had been seen by witnesses near the site where her body was found in Kintyre. Other members of the Hamilton family told us that the younger Hamilton had been a passenger in this caravanette on many occasions. He himself had been helpful but we got the feeling that he was perhaps withholding information. Despite his admissions of criminal activity with Sinclair, the team felt fairly certain that his involvement went a great deal further. How much further? That was the question.

The caravanette had become particularly significant to Operation Trinity as we examined links between Sinclair, the area where Anna's body was found and the other crime scenes. The Toyota caravanette would appear to have been Sinclair's perfect murder vehicle. It seemed no accident that the period of his ownership of this vehicle coincided with the dates of crimes we were jointly investigating.

Locating the Toyota caravanette was of huge importance to us. We knew that Sinclair had sold it on shortly after Agnes Cooney had disappeared and, through vehicle records, we began to trace all its subsequent owners. We knew that it was unlikely that a vehicle of its type, which was registered in 1976, would have survived almost thirty years. Nevertheless, we had to make every effort to trace the caravanette or any parts of it. A wealth of forensic evidence could have been hiding in its seat covers and carpets which might have linked it to Helen and Christine or any of the other crimes we were investigating. In the event, we were unlucky. All the subsequent owners of the vehicle were traced – one was even able to provide an actual photograph of it. But we eventually learned that the caravanette had survived until a few years before our inquiry. Although not registered for the road, it had lain on blocks behind the last owner's house – a restoration project that never was completed. Eventually, rust and decay took their toll and our potential forensic time capsule went to be scrapped. It was tantalisingly close but all we could do was track down carpets and materials identical to these used in the Toyota. We could use these to make comparisons with fibres found on Helen Scott's clothes but they were nothing like as good as getting our hands on the real thing would have been. However, we were able to say that there was compelling evidence that fibres found on Helen matched those from the standard fabrics used in caravanettes similar to Sinclair's one.

The caravanette posed another question. It might sound incredible but it occurred to us that Sinclair's crimes could have been committed simply because he had a means of transport. Did he execute these awful crimes simply because he could?

The murder of Anna Kenny was always going to be difficult to resolve. The length of time between her disappearance and the recovery of her body meant that there was no significant forensic evidence, but there were interesting connections.

The pub Anna left that night, the Hurdy Gurdy, was in the Townhead area of Glasgow, an area of the city Sinclair knew well. His wife's family lived in Stirling Road in Townhead in 1977 and much of the time Sinclair spent with the younger Hamilton and Gordon Hamilton would have been in this district. We also knew that Sinclair had visited the Kintyre area, where Anna's body had been found buried in her shallow grave. He had the right connections, he had the means and, most importantly, we knew he had the will to abduct and murder – he had done it before. It was compelling but it wasn't enough.

10

Two More Glasgow Killings

Taken in sequence, the next unsolved killing we examined was that of Matilda McAuley, another victim of 1977. Matilda, or Hilda as she was known, was separated from her husband and, along with her two young sons, she was living at her mother's home when she met her violent death. This is the stark summary of the facts and it doesn't begin to hint at the immediate life-shattering effect a tragedy like this has on a family. But what often also goes unrecognised is that the consequences of such heartbreak would be felt by those closest to Hilda for generations.

Hilda McAuley was a conscientious and loving parent and, like so many women in her position, to make ends meet, she had more than one job. She did cleaning work at a city-centre hairdressers' shop and at a local engineering works. Her main outlet of relaxation was going out with her friends just once a week, usually to the dancing at the famous Plaza Ballroom in Glasgow. It is one of the great sorrows of these cases that Hilda's mother Martha died while the death of her daughter was being reinvestigated. Thankfully she did live long enough to know the process had started. By the time Hilda's mum had died, in the summer of 2004, she had been told by the Operation Trinity family liaison officers that a full examination of the investigation of her daughter's death was underway.

One of the most important factors in any cold case review is the attitude of the victim's family – if there are any. On the one hand, they are often crucial to the success or otherwise of the

155

investigation. Their recollection of the events surrounding the crime can sometimes become more focused by the years and the endless thinking and rethinking about all the facts and circumstances can lead to very different perspectives from those held at the time of the crime, when emotions and passions would have been running high. Loyalties can also change and, in unsolved crimes with domestic connections, this can sometimes lead to a breakthrough. Often, though, the reopening of an old case also reopens old wounds as the hurt and the pain of what happened in the past are once again recalled. It is understandable that, for many families, the overwhelming feeling is that things are best left alone. But, for some families and friends, the continued or revitalised interest in their case is welcomed – it validates the importance of their loved one. And it sends out a powerful message that there is no such thing as an unsolved murder – the police never give up.

The families of the World's End murders never lost hope and never lost faith with the police. Neither did Martha McAuley. Her daughter's killer has not yet been brought to justice but I hope that the commitment she saw the Strathclyde team give to the reinvestigation brought her some comfort. We all hoped that our continued efforts gave her some peace of mind during her final days, after so many years of heartache.

Hilda lived with her mother in the Maryhill Road area of Glasgow. It was the district that kept cropping up during the many facets of this inquiry. It was the centre of Angus Sinclair's territory, near his former home in Daisy Street and a short walk from the scene of at least one of his attacks on children. Hilda, who was thirty-six when she died, had a bad habit – one that, in the end, may have cost her her life. For convenience, she was in the habit of accepting lifts home from men she had met after a night out in the Plaza. Sometimes they were men she didn't know. Saturday, 1 October 1977, two weeks before the World's End murders, may have been just such a night.

Hilda had gone out with the intention of ending up at 'the dancing' in the Plaza with three close friends. The four of them had met in the early evening and had a drink in a couple of pubs before arriving at the Plaza shortly after ten o'clock. Jackets were left at the upstairs cloakroom and they walked down to the dance floor where the little group parted company, as they often did on nights like this. Police would eventually trace and speak to most of the people who were in the dance hall that night and no one saw anything that stood out as unusual. It was just another Saturday night at the Plaza.

Hilda, as far as we could ascertain, spent a lot of the two hours or so that she was in the Plaza on her own. The only fix that officers were able to establish was at about quarter past midnight when the cloakroom attendant remembered Hilda reclaiming her jacket. This woman had got to know Hilda on her regular visits to the dance hall and recalled quite clearly her leaving, and told officers she appeared to be sober and showing no signs of being the worse for wear after a long evening.

Hilda had left the Plaza at about the time the place usually started to empty, with revellers heading off to catch last the buses home, so no one paid too much attention to her departure. In fact, no one remembers seeing anything of Hilda either inside the Plaza or outside after she reclaimed her jacket. We may never know exactly what happened in those moments on Sunday, 2 October 1977 after she left the dance hall. She may have been alone or she may have been with a man who was offering her one of these convenient lifts home. The next fact that we can be certain about in the story of Hilda McAuley is that she was found brutally murdered some twelve hours later. Sometime, somehow, in those moments after midnight, she met her killer and was carried away.

Hilda's body was found dumped in trees on waste ground at Langbank in Renfrewshire beside what was to become in later years a motorway. In those days, it was the main road between Glasgow and the Clydeside shipbuilding town of Greenock. The area was beside the entrance to a caravan park and was the sort of place that a vehicle could remain unnoticed for some time as traffic raced by on adjacent roads. It was an obscure spot – the kind of place that courting couples might know. It would certainly have required a degree of local knowledge both to know it was there – you wouldn't find the place by accident – and to appreciate what a good place it was for disposing of a body.

As the case of Hilda McAuley was re-examined by the Operation Trinity team, potential coincidences and significant clues emerged from the pages of the old statements they were combing through. That is not to criticise those involved in the original inquiry in any way at all. It is much easier to spot similarities if you know exactly what you are looking for. For instance, we knew by this time that Angus Sinclair owned a very distinctive white caravanette during this period so, while sightings or references to such a vehicle would be significant to us, they wouldn't have been significant to the original inquiry team, who had no leads regarding any suspect's vehicles and would have been trying to make some sense of hundreds of car descriptions, some accurate, some vague, without a clue as to the relative importance of any of them.

The small details contained in statements given at the time took on a new meaning for us as we tried to piece together the jigsaw. We had the luxury of being fairly certain what the final picture would look like. We were also aware that Sinclair knew the area well. His sister lived nearby and a former girlfriend of his told us how they used to go for runs in his car to other places very close by. We learned from one of his old criminal pals that, years before, they had travelled to a spot near Langbank for a very specific purpose. They went to test-fire a pistol that they planned to use in future crimes. The exact spot could not be identified but Sinclair's pal remembered it was littered with burnt-out cars that had been dumped as scrap or by joyriders. We knew that when Hilda's body was found the area nearby was known as a dump site for cars. It was a tantalising connection. The spot was hidden yet accessible from the roads close by. It was ideal for dumping cars or for any other activity that you wanted to go unnoticed.

Hilda's body was found by a father and his two sons out shooting rabbits at lunchtime the day after she went missing. She, like the other victims, had been bound securely, gagged and strangled. Hilda had been left partially stripped and the rest of her clothing in disarray. Some items Hilda was known to have with her when she left home to go dancing were never found. Her coat, handbag, shoes and a hairpiece were missing and they were the subject of a massive search and public appeals by the original inquiry. By the time Operation Trinity was revisiting the case, the bindings, the gag and Hilda's clothing could not be traced. It was a huge setback for we could only speculate what forensic evidence they might have yielded.

Some documents did, however, survive. The original investigation had been extensive, as had the examination by forensic experts. We were able to make full use of our predecessors' work. Some 1,200 people were interviewed in depth about the night of the disappearance but, despite this intensive operation, they had been unable to find anyone who had seen Hilda McAuley leaving the Plaza Ballroom or at any time afterwards.

Re-examining the case all these years later was, of course, made very much more difficult by the fact that none of the productions had survived the passage of time. In the World's End case, traces of DNA in items recovered from the crime scenes had led to Sinclair and Gordon Hamilton being identified. In the case of Hilda McAuley, we had no such advantage. Such was our need to trace these items that an inquiry within the inquiry was launched and the Strathclyde team painstakingly retraced the steps of the original investigators – dozens of detectives and scientists over nearly thirty years. No stone was left unturned in the examination of record books and evidence schedules. Even the old cabinets at forensic laboratories were searched. It was a magnificent effort but it yielded nothing. We even made contact with surviving detectives and scientists from 1977. This may sound like a bizarre long-shot or the plot of TV fiction but it is more valuable that you might first think. Detectives and scientists tend to remember unsolved cases. When long hours, weeks and sometimes months are devoted to individual cases, it becomes personal and you never forget the details of crimes that have become etched on your memory.

During Operation Trinity, we made great efforts to contact retired detectives and scientists who had been involved in the various cases. We had considerable assistance and I was hugely impressed by the recall and enthusiasm of these long-retired men and women. It was clear that they still felt an ownership.

By this time, the investigation into Sinclair was being progressed under three main headings. There was the probe into his connections with friends and family, including the various addresses at which he had lived as a free man. There were the vehicles he owned and lastly his links with the places where each of the victims was last seen and where their bodies were eventually found.

In the case of Hilda McAuley, the second and third strands of the investigation were coming together. We learned of a car that had been dumped in 1978 in a disused quarry near to where Hilda's body was discovered by the rabbit shooters. A huge amount of time and manpower were expended digging through the scrap and stone lying about in the former Glenboig quarry and, sure enough, Strathclyde Police's hugely experienced underwater search team found the car. Most interestingly, in the boot of the car, we found various lengths of string. Could this be the same kind of string used to bind Hilda McAuley? How would we ever know for certain while the original materials were untraced?

This string, however, provides a wonderful example of just how, with care and attention to detail, it is possible to reach back through time and discover evidence of a vital nature. The actual string from Hilda's body had gone. However, all the documentation of the original forensic investigation survived and, amongst it, there was a report from the University of Strathclyde identifying the type of string that had been used. It had been concluded that the string was of a unique manufacture. In fact, there was only one company making this particular type of string and it was in Co. Kildare, Ireland. In 1977, detectives had discovered a business in Glasgow, Henry Winning & Co. in Caroline Street, that was an outlet for the Irish string.

Then officers were hampered by a lack of suspect. When they had visited Winning's, they found that this product was sold to a large number of trades folk all over the west of Scotland. Sales were plentiful and many untraceable. Short of interviewing every person who had access to this string in every company that bought it and then checking their alibis for the night of Hilda's murder, there was no way forward. Even if only 100 balls of this string had been sold, just consider how impossible a task this would be. Not all of those balls would be traceable for a start. Then, for companies that were known to have bought the string, trying to establish exactly who would have access to it. We were more fortunate as we had a clear focus for our investigation.

So the Strathclyde team went back to reinterview the man who ran Winning's in 1977 and he recognised the string. He also recalled being interviewed by the original investigation team almost thirty years before. But what was the connection? Next Strathclyde interviewed the boss of the company Gordon Hamilton worked for about this time, a manager of the button dying firm A. M. Robb Ltd. He recalled the string and said they used it for tying up small parcels – and had purchased it from Winning's. Examination of Robb's records found bills from Winning's at this time. For good measure, a second Glasgow company that stocked the Irish twine was also checked and they too supplied Robb's with it. We even managed to find a little parcel which had lain around for all these years unopened and which was tied up with the very same twine. In the end, this is nothing but an interesting tale but the story of the string is a very good illustration of the intricacy and depth of our inquiries and how it is possible to fill in seemingly unbridgeable gaps even after nearly thirty years.

Fascinating though these details were, we could not be distracted by them for the main thrust of our investigations at this stage still centred on a detailed re-examination of the five murders, looking at them in the fresh light provided by having a good suspect for two of them – Angus Sinclair for the World's End ones.

What we initially thought was the last in the series of killings was that of Agnes Cooney. She was a 23-year-old house parent at a children's home in Bellshill, Lanarkshire, on the outskirts of Glasgow. Agnes was, by all accounts, one of life's caring individuals who took her responsibilities very seriously and went out of her way to help those in need. The last photograph of her shows a cheery, cheeky face full of life and fun.

She was just seventeen years old when her mother and grandmother both died during 1971 and the young Agnes took on the mother role to her five younger brothers and sisters at their home in Coatbridge, Lanarkshire. Everyone who knew her spoke of how well she carried out this difficult surrogate role. Words like 'strong', 'dependable' and 'fiercely protective' were used to describe Agnes.

To fulfil this caring role, Agnes had had to put her ambition to become a nurse on hold so she could stay at home where she was needed. But Agnes also found time to work at a department store in Glasgow until her younger brothers and sisters were older and independent. That day came soon enough, though, and it would have been with great excitement that Agnes gave up her job at Bremner's store in Glasgow city centre to begin her nursing training at a hospital in Mauchline in Ayrshire, living in the nurses' home nearby.

The caring, committed nature of Agnes's personality is clear from the original statements and reports compiled by officers after her murder in December 1977. This kindly disposition had led her to take up a job as a house parent at a children's home in Lanarkshire when she completed her nursing training and that was the job she was doing when she was killed.

Agnes also spent some of her spare time at a house in Glasgow looking after an aged aunt. She was staying at this address at the time she was murdered. Her father died without the satisfaction of seeing his daughter's killer brought to justice. Her brothers and sisters survive and are still deeply affected by the tragedy.

As in all these cases, the events leading up to the murder were unexceptional – normal people leading normal lives only brought into prominence by a chance meeting with a brutal murderer. On the day she vanished, Agnes had been to see a flat she was considering renting in the Maryhill area of Glasgow with a friend. The pair had done their nursing training together and had become very good friends. Agnes's potential flatmate was going out with a man who was a member of a local band and he joined the two young women as they viewed the flat. The three went on to have supper together at a city centre restaurant and eventually made their way to a club where the band was due to play that night.

The two girls helped the young musician and other members of his band as they unloaded their gear into the Cladda Club in Westmoreland Street in the city centre. After they had set up their amplifiers and speakers, Agnes and her friend settled down to watch the show until it finished in the club about 11 p.m. With the entertainment over, the girls once more lent a hand and lugged instruments and amps back out to the band's van, which was parked outside.

A band member told detectives in 1977 that, as they were packing up, he'd noticed a white Transit-like van with windows at the rear parked across the road. It had taken about fifty minutes or so to load up the band's van and, just before midnight, Agnes was seen leaving the Cladda Club by herself. She seemed to be perfectly normal. She was not upset and had appeared happy as she wished staff goodnight. Not long afterwards, the band members and Agnes's pal realised she had gone without saying goodbye and they were concerned she had just wandered off in an area of Glasgow that was not well known to her.

Agnes's friends first looked round the club and then moved outside to see if they could spot her in the street or standing at a bus stop. There was no sign of her. Later there was a sighting of someone looking very much like Agnes walking in the city centre. Witnesses were to describe her clothing very precisely, leaving officers in no doubt that the sighting was of Agnes walking off into the night and that she was quite alone.

Glasgow is bisected by the M8 motorway and, on either side of it, there are areas of wasteland between the road and the shops and houses. The next series of possible sightings of Agnes were all either on or near this busy route. She appeared to be trying to hitch a lift. There were numerous reports of a woman seen in various locations round the M8. Much of this no-man's-land is made up of a series of underpasses and slip roads which can be daunting enough in daytime but are no place for a young woman alone in the early hours of the morning. Officers worked on the basis that these sightings were of Agnes and they continued to receive further reports of sightings of the lone woman over the next hour or more after she'd left the club. The last was from a motorist who saw someone who may have been Agnes at about 2 a.m. We will never know if any or all of these sighting were really of Agnes. In the clamour of publicity following a high-profile murder, there can be many well-intentioned but misleading reports of potential sightings. If it was Agnes, her behaviour was as untypical as it was dangerous. Walking alone in a strange part of town in the dark was risky behaviour for a young woman and Agnes was not a risk taker.

The band members and friends eventually gave up their searches and, believing nothing was seriously wrong, they went their separate ways. What had been puzzling for her friends turned to outright concern when Agnes failed to turn up at work the next morning. Her absence sparked a series of frantic phone calls to friends and family but all drew a blank as to her whereabouts. Eventually the decision was made to raise the alarm and Agnes was reported missing to the police on the afternoon of Saturday, 3 December 1977.

She did not remain a missing person for long. At nine o'clock on the morning of Sunday the 4th, her body was found on farmland near Caldercruix in Lanarkshire. A local farmer was driving his tractor along a minor road past his fields when he saw what he took to be a bundle of rags lying about fifteen yards out into the grass. As he continued to drive along the narrow road, it slowly dawned on him that it was probably not just rags but a human body. He raced to his neighbour's farmhouse and raised the alarm. On returning with his neighbour, they confirmed that it was indeed a body lying in the field and the police were called. The farmer told officers he had been working in the area where the body was discovered throughout the previous day and so was certain it had not been there when he'd finished on the Saturday.

Agnes had been bound and gagged with items of her own clothing. The gag was no longer in place when the body was found but the bindings that had been used to hold it in place were still tied round her mouth. She had died from a stab wound.

There was a clear suggestion she may have been alive for a considerable period of time in between her disappearance from Glasgow city centre in the early hours of Saturday morning and the time she was killed. Had she been kept somewhere for that twenty-four to thirty-six hours and, if so, where?

Again there was an extensive police inquiry into the killing. It must have seemed fairly obvious to detectives in those days that, if it had been Agnes trying to hitch a lift on or near the M8, in all likelihood, a man had picked her up and he was the one who had killed her. No one came forward to say they had seen her getting into a car and there were no significant sightings at the time of the vehicle that must have been used to dump her body in this relatively remote spot. For our inquiry in 2004, the profile was very similar to the rest. Again none of the original evidential productions or samples from the initial inquiry had survived the passage of time so we were going to have to go back through this investigation with a fine-tooth comb. Armed with our most recent information, we would have to reinterview surviving witnesses to see if we could add to the knowledge gathered at the time of the original inquiry.

Key amongst our lines of inquiry was the sighting of a newish white van being driven in the vicinity of the deposition site on the Saturday night. Like so many people in major inquiries, the witness had not thought his information important which is why he had delayed in coming forward. By the time he had contacted police, the case of Agnes Cooney was receiving considerable press coverage and even at that stage it was being linked by reporters to the earlier killings and particularly the World's End murders. The press were beginning to notice the similarities and coming to their own conclusions.

Back then, of course, the white van was just one of many different vehicles people had reported seeing in various places and so it would have been treated accordingly. But, for us, it was extremely important because, when Agnes died, we knew that the vehicle Sinclair was driving was a white Toyota caravanette and it was new.

Yet another of the significant developments came to Operation Trinity as a result of the publicity surrounding our inquiries and the speculation that we were interested in Sinclair. On 31 October 1977, a nine-year-old girl was the victim of a sex assault near her home in Glasgow. The attack had been reported to the police when it happened but no culprit was ever identified. In 2001, after Sinclair's conviction for the murder of Mary Gallagher, the victim, a woman I will call 'Joan', again contacted the police, saying she believed Sinclair was the man who attacked her all those years ago. This case was very important. The attack on Joan, at the end of October 1977, was not only a very serious crime, it also marked a change in offending behaviour.

When we first identified Sinclair as one of the individuals involved in the World's End murders and learned of his later convictions for offences against much younger girls, the crimes for which he was first sentenced to life imprisonment, we wondered why he had changed victim types – what had motivated the change from adult to child victims. The attack on Joan may have been the transitional crime. Horrific though the experience must have been, in hindsight, Joan was fortunate to survive.

It is clear Sinclair's offending took on a whole new direction after this time although quite why is rather difficult to speculate on. However, it is certain that, during 1977–8, he was driven to murder women. Helen Scott, Christine Eadie and Mary Gallagher – and there may have been others – were all approached late on a Friday or Saturday night, in or after leaving licensed premises, before being abducted and killed. Plus the way they were all killed bore distinctive similarities. But the attack on Joan heralded an intense period of offending against children and these new victims put him into a very different category of offender. The change from being a rapist and murderer of women to becoming a violent child sex attacker happened very suddenly.

So what brought it about? In the absence of hard evidence, we can only speculate. Things were changing in Sinclair's life which may have brought about the alteration in his offending pattern. In the face of the publicity about a white van in the weeks after Agnes Cooney's murder, he sold the white caravanette which probably had been an essential factor in the World's End cases. Worried that eventually the police might identify it, he may have felt it was getting too hot. Whatever he was thinking, the vehicle was certainly sold on very soon after Agnes's death.

With the loss of his transport, he might have decided to turn his attention to children because they would have been easier to subdue and control and he would not have needed his van to hold them in. It is sometimes the simplest of things that bring about major events. Sinclair's change in behaviour may have been merely about the loss of his caravanette.

The tenement close where Joan was attacked was just 200 yards from Sinclair's home at Daisy Street and not far from either the Cladda Club or the Plaza Ballroom. It was right in the centre of Sinclair's territory. And the case bore many familiar hallmarks. The little girl had been wandering the streets of her home district, waiting for her father to come home and let her into their tenement flat. He was a heavy drinker and Joan often spent hours hanging around waiting for him to roll home from the pub. That day in October 1977, a man had approached her and asked for help in finding a family called Thomson. Ever happy to help, the little girl took on the task and tried two nearby families of that name but discovered neither was expecting a visitor. She returned to the man she later identified as Sinclair with this information. He then asked her to go to another street with him and, once there, he sent her into an unlit tenement close again in search of the mythical Thomson family who, he said, probably lived on the top floor. She climbed the stairs and, on discovering no one of that name there, began walking back down the dark stair to be met by her attacker on the second floor. There he grabbed her, pinned her to the wall and threatened her with a knife. He then subjected the girl to a terrifying ordeal. Afraid her assailant would kill her, she was crying as quietly as she could and, as the attack continued, she was biting the sleeve of her anorak to stop herself from screaming out loud.

After a while, she heard the front door of the close, two floors below, open. Her attacker jumped up and rearranged his clothing. He then ordered the petrified girl to go to the top landing and not tell anyone what had happened. The man who had entered the close found Joan crying. With her clothing in disarray, it was obvious she had been attacked by the man who had just passed him on the stairs a couple of floors below. He banged on the door of a flat and then ran off to try to catch her attacker but to no avail.

No one was ever charged with this attack. Joan told officers in 2001 that she had gone to an identification parade but had been too frightened to pick out her attacker, if indeed he had even been in the line-up.

Another consequence of this awful experience was that Joan was taken into care on the night of the attack when police found her father drunk and incapable of looking after her. She spent the rest of her childhood in the care of the local council.

Again no productions from this case had survived – and, this time, even the paperwork had disappeared over the years. When Joan came forward after seeing Sinclair's case in the papers, she was able to give a very full recollection of what had happened and even picked Sinclair's picture out of a large collection of photographs she was shown.

Given the terror of the attack and the tragic family consequences that followed, it says much for this young woman's character that, despite the passage of time, many of the details of that dreadful day were still firmly in her mind, including one that was of special interest to us. She recalled her attacker's trousers had flecks of paint on them.

Reading this case in 2004, the similarities hit us like a sledge hammer. The circumstances and the modus operandi were identical to those of another case we were very familiar with. If you change the names and the dates, you could have been reading the Catherine Reehill case from 1961. The crimes were almost identical with only one important difference – Joan survived.

During the long hours of interviews with Sinclair into various aspects of the case being built up against him, he said little and revealed nothing. When questioned in December 2004 about the attack on Joan, Sinclair was read the girl's account of what had happened to her and, as usual, he gave not the slightest flicker of a reaction to that graphic document. Uniquely, in this instance, he did break from his usual 'no comment' stance to concede what had happened to the little girl had been 'quite horrendous'. Cool, detached and cynical? Or could this have been the good Angus Sinclair passing judgement on the bad one?

11

Confronting the Suspect

Every single detail of Operation Trinity was important in its own way. Each order, each inquiry, each review of evidence became another block in the process of building a strong case aimed at bringing justice in these historic cases after a quarter of a century of frustration. Apart from the DNA evidence, no other part of this investigation was potentially more important than the interviews we would conduct with Sinclair.

We had come a long way since my early days in the CID, when it was often a case of accusation and denial until, hopefully, the suspect gave up. Some of the old detectives were masters at winning the psychological battle with suspects. Their techniques differed – some would show the interviewee empathy, others would use the classic good-cop-bad-cop routine and, in the distant past, it might have been the case of resorting to physical intimidation and brute force. They all worked with some people in some circumstances but, even if the suspect did crack or better still sign a confession in a police notebook, it would usually be retracted on advice of a lawyer and the subsequent court appearance descended into a series of accusations of fabrication and denial. Before the 60s, it was usually straightforward and the court simply accepted the officer's version as a witness of stature and credibility – end of story. But it started to change after the corruption inquiries in the Metropolitan area in the 1960s. The credibility of the police was never quite the same again and later revelations from the West Midlands Serious

Crime Squad and many others did nothing to help. These cases of malpractice, corner-cutting and 'fitting-up' were self-inflicted wounds and all were hugely damaging to the entire police service – trust was gone.

In Scotland, mainly because of our unique rules of corroboration, major problems were avoided and there were fewer scandals. Nonetheless, the world had changed and it soon became the case that admissions in Scottish criminal cases were viewed with suspicion, times of detention were restricted and we all had to get a little more professional. It became important that any admission contained specialist knowledge – in other words, something that only the culprit could know such as the location of the body, the stolen goods or the weapon. In such circumstances, the specialist knowledge and the consequent recovery of the evidence were usually persuasive enough to give the confession some credibility.

There were, of course, ways round this as there are with most safeguards but, for the most part, the tightening of the rules, while despised by some old cops, was good for everyone. It offered protection for the innocent suspect who was in the wrong place at the wrong time, forced the police officer to prepare more thoroughly and not simply depend on a verbal admission, and it also protected younger officers from the pressure of older colleagues to 'get a result'.

Had Angus Sinclair been arrested for the World's End killings in the 1970s, the interviews would have been thorough but crude by comparison to the techniques of the twenty-first century. Nowadays, for serious cases, interviews are at least tape-recorded and more often videoed as well. They are the subject of intense preparation and nothing is left to chance. In Sinclair's case, as in other major inquiries, the police are governed by very strict rules of interview, the breaking of which can render any material gathered inadmissible and worthless. This could not be allowed to happen in our case. Sinclair's long experience of the criminal justice system meant he would be very unlikely to be overawed or intimidated by the process. The fact that we had to go public on the investigation many months before seeing him for the first time also meant the element of surprise was gone and he had plenty of time to think things over and prepare for our eventual arrival.

The exceptional circumstances we were dealing with in Sinclair's case meant we needed an exceptional approach to these crucial interviews that, given the number of crimes we were investigating, would stretch over many sessions. He would be questioned about the murders, of course, but also about the robberies and assaults we pulled from the files. A huge planning process was put into establishing a strategy, selecting interviewing officers, training them for the different responses they might get from Sinclair, gathering and collating what are known as interview aids, maps, photographs, sketches to help jog the memory and of course demonstrate the degree of care that has gone into our inquiry.

Early on in Operation Trinity, we turned for help once more to the National Crime and Operations Faculty and got the help of a top criminal psychologist. We had to make sure we were going to get the maximum benefit from the time-limited sessions spent interviewing Sinclair. It wouldn't be right to name the psychologist who helped us but she was one of the best – hugely experienced in the field, she had a long track record of success in dealing with Britain's most dangerous criminals. She was able to form opinions of Sinclair from videoed interviews conducted in 2000 when he had been questioned over the murder of Mary Gallagher. After she'd reviewed each interview the police had conducted with him back then, she made observations and offered guidance on tactics and further plans of action.

We first met Angus Sinclair in a videoed meeting in October of 2004 at Peterhead Prison. The aim of the initial interview was to introduce him to the investigation, give him details of how we saw it progressing over the future weeks and explain to him what his involvement would be. This may seem rather odd to those not acquainted with modern police procedures – a little too polite perhaps. In fact, this approach was suggested as a method of overcoming one of Sinclair's personality traits – one that might stand in the way of successful questioning. Broadly speaking, our psychologist observed that, in the past, Sinclair had been able to take some control of police interviews. He used his self-discipline and contempt for the entire process to intimidate interviewing officers and dominate the exchanges. He also used all sorts of tricks to exasperate interviewing officers to the point where they lost any chance of obtaining meaningful progress. We saw how Sinclair used his eyes very effectively to turn the direction of the interview. He would stare at interviewers in such a way as to make them feel uncomfortable. The inexperienced or unprepared inter-locutor would soon find himself on the defensive. The questioning process of a suspect is a fascinating drama of human interaction and role-play which, if entered into by either side with unjustified confidence, can lead to disaster. Take, for example, the cocky criminal who thinks he can easily outsmart the police – often you find his tongue gets the better of him and he contradicts himself or makes unintentional admissions as his guard fails. Once that happens, the game is up. Thankfully, most criminals are not very bright or well prepared and often the stress of the event gets to them.

However, the hardened offender who has had years to mull over his story and perfect his replies is a different challenge altogether. Add to that the time lag, Sinclair's controlling personality and his all too obvious ability to deceive and it's easy to appreciate just how difficult we believed the challenge ahead of us was going to be.

One important part of the plan was to select the right officers to carry out the interviews. Many factors had to be taken into consideration. It was important that the interviewers were experienced but we felt too much experience might work against us. They could not be so set in their ways that they would decline any advice about overcoming the particular difficulties presented by Sinclair. Nor could they be too senior. In TV police dramas, it's usually the senior detective who confronts the suspect but this is one area where fact and fiction are miles apart. It's a myth. It would have been ridiculous for me or one of the senior officers from the squad to carry out the interview. For one thing, too senior an officer gives an impression of status or importance to the suspect. To an egotist like Sinclair, this would have been a gift and a mistake for us. But there was another, more practical reason for my non-involvement. The truth was that my interviewing skills were rusty and my techniques well out of date. The other senior officers were more recently practised but still not as proficient as middle-ranking operational detectives whose experience was current and techniques bang uptodate. In all major case interviews, it is experience, skill and suitability that count, not rank or seniority.

Despite the weight of the forensic evidence that we had, the interview with Sinclair was of the utmost importance and, after careful consideration and lengthy discussions with Ian Thomas and Eddie McCusker, we picked one officer from Strathclyde and one from Lothian and Borders. We felt they offered the necessary experience and the ability to represent us best. Detective Sergeants Calum Young and Jim Shanley may not at first have welcomed their selection as interviewing officers – after all, it was a huge responsibility with a lot resting on the outcome. Naturally they gave no indication one way or the other but they certainly knew that the whole squad was relying on them. The simple truth was that, in the near thirty years of the inquiry, the thousands of jobs undertaken and the hundreds of detectives who had gone before, they were the first to be able to look the World's End suspect in the eye – it would be both a great opportunity and a weighty responsibility. They may have been apprehensive but we were certain we had picked the correct lead interviewers. Both officers had good reputations and the right skills for the job.

It was unlikely that the sheer power and eloquence of the interview would bring about a change of heart in the suspect to the extent that he would make a full and frank confession, but it certainly was the case that any future prosecution would, in all probability, rely heavily on the videotapes of the interviews to allow the jury perhaps their only chance of hearing Sinclair's story in his own words and form a judgement on it. In a case like this, the accused very often decides, on legal advice, not to give evidence in court. They know how fatally damaging a good cross-examination can be. Instead, they rely on their counsel saying to the jury something like, 'There is no need for my client to go into the witness box as the prosecution have failed miserably to make a case.' While we were not to know it at the time, this is exactly what happened. Thankfully, given the opportunity, the members of a jury, who often have little legal knowledge but plenty of common sense, usually see this tactic for what it is – a device to keep the accused person from being tested or revealing his guilt in front of their eyes.

The approach we made to Sinclair would be crucial. We had to judge the situation carefully and weigh up all the various conflicting factors. We had to get it right first time.

The press, of course, had given wide coverage to our operation and inevitably Sinclair's name had been linked to the inquiry as the main suspect right from the day we first revealed the operation's existence. We were concerned that this speculation and the naming of Sinclair had continued in some of the tabloids despite warnings by the Crown Office. Surprise was going to play no part in our strategy.

From the start we had been gathering information about our suspect's life behind bars and a picture was beginning to emerge. It seemed to us that, in the mind of our suspect, there were two very separate Angus Sinclairs. One was the man of the past – the convicted murderer and sex offender – and the other was the man of the present – a man with a mission, a trusted prison worker, the master of his kitchen and the mentor of his fellow prisoners. By all accounts, Sinclair had indeed become a respected elder statesman among his peers – someone whose advice was sought and usually taken as he oversaw their meals during the long prison days.

Peterhead Prison is full of sex offenders so he had no fear of the rough justice sometimes handed out to 'the beasts' by other prisoners in the mainstream jails. Everyone in that prison was in the same boat, more or less. It was a relatively safe environment and Sinclair, by virtue of his length of service and his hard work, had risen to be first among equals.

In an effort to create the optimal conditions, we had a letter delivered to Sinclair in his cell explaining that, later that day, we would be calling to speak to him. Our psychologist had been struck by his courtesy and was convinced that treating him with the same level of courtesy as he offered was the best way forward. The interview sessions stretching out in front of us would be long, detailed and tiring. That was on the basis of him not co-operating. If he began making disclosures, then we faced an even longer but more rewarding task.

Sergeants Young and Shanley took to their brief well later that afternoon when they sat down in an interview room in the prison and patiently spelled out what was going to happen. They called him 'Mr Sinclair' or sometimes 'Sir' and he responded as our experts had anticipated. Sitting quietly and seeming relaxed, he made appropriate responses to the initial preamble, saying he understood what was going on. After a while, Calum went on to outline the details of the inquiry and how they affected him. I have watched this section of video over and over again, trying to see if there was even the slightest reaction to any of the information that was being given to him. There was not. First Sinclair was told that he was not suspected of any involvement in the two Dundee murders that had been part of Operation Trinity in the early days but quickly discounted. This was important. If Sinclair felt we were on a fishing trip – a speculative interview accusing him of crimes he knew he did not commit – he would conclude that our evidence was thin and sit back. If, on the other hand, we convinced him of the depth of our knowledge and we were right, there was a chance, albeit a very small one, that he might speak. Then there was another matter – we wanted to demonstrate our fairness and respect for him by showing that we were not simply trying to clear our books of unsolved cases. Judging by his previous interview behaviour, our chances were slim but we had to try our professional best.

Having told Sinclair the police were not linking him to the killings in Dundee, Calum then said that he was, however, suspected of being involved in other killings – ones that had taken place in Edinburgh and elsewhere in Scotland. 'Do you understand?' Calum asked him. 'Yes,' Sinclair replied in a quiet voice that betrayed no emotion. His single-word answer would be about as revealing as any we would get during what would eventually amount to many hours of detailed interviews.

Sinclair quickly told the officers that he had taken advice from a local solicitor who had instructed him to say that he had no further comment to make on any of the allegations or questions being put to him. Jim and Calum did not let this put them off and, bearing in mind the training they had gone through to help them deal with just such a 'no comment' response, they kept going to plan, reminding him every now and then that, if he really wasn't involved in the matters they were asking him about, he should say so clearly or it could potentially damage his position at any subsequent trial. We were obliged in fairness to do this, remembering that every word, inflection and nuance was being recorded by sensitive video and audio recordings, but it was also a technique to get him talking. The second word is always easier than the first – if you can get a suspect to speak, even if it is just to deny something, that is preferable by far to a stony silence. That way, there is at least some communication and with it comes the chance of a slip-up or something that can be proved to be a lie.

We also thought it important to spell out in simple terms to Sinclair how the sands had shifted over the passage of time. We needed to let him see that people who might have been his friends or allies when he was committing crimes all those years ago were no longer on his side – instead, they were now helping us in a way they would not have dreamt of a quarter of a century or more before.

We hoped to take advantage of Sinclair's comparative isolation over the years. He was no longer in control of his domestic environment, his relatives or his friends. He must have been uncertain about what changes could have taken place and we judged that, for a man with a controlling personality like Sinclair's, this would be uncomfortable.

The interviewers dropped into the conversations details from a statement his sister had made about how he had visited while she was on holiday in Cumbria. There was no great significance in this information other than it demonstrated to him the detail of our inquiry. We also let it be known that members of his wife's family had helped us gather certain information we needed. We wanted him to understand that, for the Hamilton family, covering up for a petty thief was one thing to but helping a sex killer evade justice was not on their agenda.

However, despite the very best efforts of Jim and Calum, it was all to no avail – Sinclair made it clear he was not going to say anything. He was cool, collected and in control and we had little option but to conclude the interview. It was, I suppose, something of a triumph of hope over experience to have expected anything else. A veteran prisoner with something to gain and nothing to lose is hardly likely to invite us to roll the tape for a full confession. But there was a chance he might have done exactly that. He was, after all, serving two life sentences anyway. He was already fifty-nine years old and unlikely ever to be released. What else could they do to him? Even if he had confessed and been convicted of more murders, he would have remained in his comfort zone at Peterhead. Indeed, further convictions may have enhanced his prison reputation in a twisted way. But Angus Sinclair was not that kind of man. The only confessions in his life had come when he was very young or being influenced by his wife and thoughts of family. He had learned his lesson and no such leverage existed now. In short, Angus Sinclair was not the confessing type. He would control the situation by silence. As the interviews progressed, first at Fraserburgh police station, then in Glasgow's Govan police station and finally at Livingston, the station that had provided headquarters facilities for Operation Trinity, there were to be just a very few clues given along the way.

The biggest of those was at Livingston, some considerable way into the proceedings when we had little to lose. We told Sinclair he was to be questioned over a much earlier killing, the 1970 murder of Helen Kane. This girl had been murdered in Edinburgh some years before the time we believed Sinclair to be active. However, there was a slight connection as, at one time, Sinclair had lived near the area where Helen Kane was last seen. Rather startlingly, he replied to the effect that it was nothing to do with him. He was precise and clear, declaring adamantly, 'This one is nothing to do with me.' By going further than he had during countless hours of interviews over several months, Sinclair gave us the first real response. Helen Kane's death may have had nothing to do with him but, in saying so, he gave the impression that the other cases may well have been his handiwork. It is, of course, difficult to know exactly what to read into that comment. Was it a fatal slip in an unguarded moment or the natural response of an innocent man or something more subtle? Whatever the reason, it is interesting to contrast this response with the utter silence and detachment of the previous interviews and his performance when he was interviewed about the vicious attack on the rent collector at Moodiesburn – a crime we knew he carried out with his younger brother-in-law.

The investigation was based in the Central Belt so, after the interview sessions at Fraserburgh had been completed, it made practical sense to transfer Sinclair from Peterhead to Barlinnie in Glasgow. The general pattern of all these interview attempts was the same. He'd be detained under Section 14 of the Criminal Procedure (Scotland) Act and, by the time of the interview at Govan in late November 2004, he was being held in Barlinnie, traditionally one of the toughest prisons in Scotland. As well as moving him for practical reasons, we had also hoped that the change of scene might unnerve Sinclair. He would no longer be in the safe and relatively comfortable surroundings he was used to and in which he enjoyed status and respect. He may have felt nervous, anxious and even vulnerable but, if he did, he certainly didn't show it. He appeared to settle into Barlinnie within hours of his arrival and, after just a few days, he had made such a favourable impression with prison staff that he had won a position of respect. In exactly the same way as he had done at Peterhead, he was working the system perfectly.

So, as usual, manners and courtesy were to the fore as Calum Young, this time with another Strathclyde officer, Joe McKerns, sat down in the interview room at Govan and began the standard formalities. With his name, age and address all noted, a full explanation of the reason for this interview was given. Yes, he understood what they were asking him about. Yes, he understood that, as usual, there were people watching the interview live in another room in the police station. And that was it. His stock reply to any question was 'nothing further to say' and he even trotted it out in response to being asked if he knew where Moodiesburn was.

The officers were anxious to move him on from that, the feeling

181

being that even the slightest deviation from his plan may start a little trickle of information that would grow. Once they had established that there was to be no response to the questions over the detail of that terrifying robbery in Moodiesburn, the pair of officers switched to a different tack. They began to ask him exactly why it was that he had nothing further to say. In their drive in this direction, Joe and Calum suggested, ever so gently, that Sinclair may not be able to understand what they were asking him about – that they had somehow lost him. They would, ever so politely and apparently unintentionally, question his intellect – give him the impression that they thought he wasn't quite with it. They would leave him feeling he had to say something to assert himself and show that he was in charge of the interview, not them – that the session was on his terms not theirs. It was worth a try but it did not work. All he would say was something like, 'I understand what you are saying and the response will be that I have nothing further to say.'

And so it went on. They asked why he was saying that he had nothing further to say and got the stock reply. By doing this, he said he was only following the advice of his solicitor. When he was challenged about not having spoken to his solicitor that day and reminded that his solicitor didn't even know he was at the police station being questioned, it made no difference – the rebuff was the same. Throughout this fairly lengthy session, his patience only seemed tried on a couple of occasions. 'Please don't badger me all day,' he said, 'I have nothing further to say.' Knowing the camera and the tape would pick up every nuance, he delivered this remark in a quiet, measured tone.

During those interviews, we deliberately showed Sinclair just exactly how much work had gone into Operation Trinity and made sure he was aware of how much we knew about him, his associates and his habits over the years. For instance, he had been involved with a man I will call James Smith, who had employed Sinclair for a time in his car repair business. Smith had spoken extensively to us about our suspect. He mentioned how Sinclair had once told him that the best way to pick up a woman was simply to approach one in the street. Indeed, Smith said he had actually been in Sinclair's car when he stopped and offered a lift to a woman walking alone in the street at night. But, no matter what was introduced, what details we revealed, he remain unflustered and seemingly unconcerned. Always polite, he was apparently content to sit there for as long as we wanted and showed no frustration or irritation at our continuing questions.

Bizarrely, he was even reluctant to discuss a cut on his face. Calum had started to ask him about his general appearance. It was just another attempt to get him talking about anything but it was based on Calum's keen observation. He had noticed that Sinclair had arrived in the police station with his shoelaces undone. It was no big deal but it did seem rather odd for a man who, until that point, had been fastidious about his appearance. When asked why he hadn't tied his laces, Sinclair had nothing further to say about it. Then Calum mentioned the cut on his face – had he done it shaving and, if so, when? 'I have nothing further to say,' said Sinclair so Calum gave him a little verbal nudge to underline the ridiculousness of this stance on such a trivial matter. It worked. With slight embarrassment, Sinclair revealed that he had cut himself shaving the previous morning. There was no breakthrough though, no connection. After this momentary frankness, it was just back to the usual silence.

As this session built towards a climax, Joe laid it on the line to Sinclair – friends from long ago were not friends any more. To underline that point, he slowly and clearly read Sinclair a lengthy extract from his co-accused's confession to the Moodiesburn robbery without identifying the source of the information. There was no hint of a reaction to this – no change in demeanour or expression. So Joe went on to ask Sinclair who he thought could have made the statement. When Joe supplied the answer, it was met with apparent indifference from the suspect.

As the questions continued, the officers made it clear to him they would not stop. The questions would go on for weeks or months until they got the answers they needed. Joe cut to the chase. Sinclair should realise his family were helping the police and the detectives of Operation Trinity had built up a massive case against him.

Joe pointed out that, as he had been putting all these matters to Sinclair, the prisoner had allowed himself 'a wee wry smile'. Why was this? Was it because he knew he did have something further to say or was it because of his disdain for the witnesses' courage in coming forward and saying the things they had? But, as the heat was turned up, Sinclair remained resolute. 'I have nothing further to say' was, by this time, his mantra and it was to be his only response.

The frustration of these interviews must be evident to all. They are, however, vitally important to an investigation of this nature. They give us lots of clues and indications if not real answers. Importantly, though, in court much can eventually be made of the fact that the accused was offered the chance to rebut the allegations and chose not to. Questions can legitimately be asked of his version of events in his own defence. 'If such and such was the case, why did you not tell the officers at the time of interview all those months ago?' It is a question a jury has the right to hear asked and answered if Sinclair were ever to go into the witness box at a trial. In the event, Sinclair never had to explain himself or account for the fact that his DNA had been found on two murdered girls.

As I have said, the preparations for these question-and-answer sessions were extremely detailed and well thought through. The questioning officers were changed and all had preparations with carefully briefed officers playing the role of Sinclair to allow the interview teams to gather experience of handling whichever tactics the suspect chose to deploy.

The first of the major sessions took place on 18 November 2004 in the police station in Fraserburgh, along the coast from Peterhead. All too often in the police – and, indeed, in most other walks of life – important operations fall short of expectations because the details have not been properly thought through or the apparently little things have been left to chance. We were determined this would not be the case here and a detailed order was drawn up over a period of days and considered very carefully.

The car used to take Sinclair from prison to police office was wired so that his conversation with accompanying officers could be recorded. This wasn't anything underhand – he was warned in advance this had been done. Thought had been given to the people involved and their likely interaction with Sinclair and so officers were told exactly which seats to occupy in the car – who was next to him and which officer sat in front.

The interviewing officers, in this case Calum and Joe again, had a detailed interview plan with all the areas to be covered carefully laid out and structured. The vehicles owned by Sinclair were very important to the investigation and so we managed to get pictures of their insides and outsides by tracing people who owned them after Sinclair and, with their help, searching through family photograph albums. The vehicle we were most interested in, of course, was the caravanette that he had owned during the period of these murders. It was the vehicle we had been told he used for his weekend fishing trips with Gordon – the trips that took up the whole weekend but never seemed to produce any fish.

So, after the tape-recorder and video camera were turned on, he was told the subject of this day's session – one of the Glasgow murders. Things took a depressingly familiar direction. 'I have nothing further to say' was once more the best we could extract. Until, that is, we got on to the subject of his cars and, for once, he seemed engaged and curious – almost forthcoming. It was truly remarkable. Here we had a man who was determined to hide the dreadful secrets of his past, particularly the serious sex offences, yet, for some reason, he started talking about the cars he owned. Sinclair must have known the vehicles he drove, particularly the caravanette, would be a significant part of our inquiry. He is, when all is said and done, a clever man who knew our investigations had stretched back through time to unearth huge volumes of new evidence relating directly to him. He had little or no idea of what we had discovered and he had no way of knowing just how important it was for us to establish which cars he owned and when, and yet here he was speaking for the first time as if he was enjoying the recollection – fondly remembering his pride and joy.

In the first part of the interview that day, he stuck rigidly to 'I have nothing further to say' even to the point that, at one stage, he burst out laughing as he said it and then apologised for doing so. This indicated to us that the scene was beginning to take on something of the ridiculous even to him. After a break he spoke a couple of sentences about his jail work, in the kitchens at Peterhead, then stopped himself and, as if reproaching himself, asked for the interview to be cut short because he was saying nothing more.

So there we have him – disciplined, focused and determined not to talk lest he gives away even the slightest clue that may crack the facade and prompt further revelations. Then, slowly but surely, information started to dribble from him. There was no consistency in his approach. In one question, he would refuse to say even where his son had gone to school and then, in his next answer, he would go into a little detail. Calum Young and Sinclair ended up doing a verbal dance as, little by little, more and more was squeezed out of him. We weren't getting far and we were certainly nowhere near a confession – no hints of admissions – but there was a steady trickle of information that allowed us to confirm various minor matters we had been less than certain of and, perhaps more importantly, this allowed Sinclair to realise just how much detail of his life was in our possession. We were able to sit and go through his tax records with him. These clearly showed where he was working and when.

Perhaps, for once, the control freak in him slipped a little and, on being confronted with overwhelming evidence on minor matters, he felt comfortable in agreeing with the facts as they were presented to him and, forgetting for a moment to shut up, he sometimes even added a little to what we already knew. Throughout this slightly more productive session, he kept falling back on his 'no further comment' line and then, almost in the same breath, he'd make further comment.

For his interviewers, it must have been extremely difficult to continue with those lengthy sessions and stick to the methods they'd been trained to use when they were up against a wall of silence or a repeated response of 'no comment'. Their task must have frustrating and at times demoralising so, on the few occasions when Sinclair did open up, the officers would have found it a welcome break.

It went further still. The exact details of the interviews are relatively unimportant but they deserve further examination if only to establish why we progressed on that particular day. Calum started asking about the places he lived in and inevitably that brought in his wife. He agreed that he spent lengthy periods of time separated while they were married and admitted that he took up with other women during these periods. Perhaps deep down a little phrase Calum used at the start of this conversation struck a chord with Sinclair and make him think differently about his situation. Remember that, from the start, we had been at great pains to demonstrate that the people he once regarded as friends and allies may have switched allegiance. One of his accomplices, his partner in the non-sexual crimes, had gone as far as to make formal statements implicating himself in serious offences, such was the change in relationships over the passage of time.

Calum emphasised once more the extent of the investigations we had conducted into his past and told him that we had spoken to a great many of the women he had known over the years. He then told Sinclair that a lot of the women still held him in 'great fondness'. Perhaps this little phrase was sufficient to bring about a bit of a sea change in Sinclair's attitude. Before this moment, the interviewing officers, over all the sessions they had conducted, had given the impression to Sinclair that he was on his own, friendless and alone. Now here were the police telling him some of his old girlfriends still regarded him well.

When he was asked about one of his more long-standing girl-friends, he agreed that he did know her. He said the flat she stayed in wasn't a very nice place and it had no heating or electricity. Then the shutters came down again and questions about her were met with the usual 'no comment' reply.

He was then asked about his friend James Smith. Smith was important to us because he told how his mother's house in Moodiesburn was being painted by Sinclair at the time of the rent collector assault and robbery that we knew he and his younger brother-in-law had carried out just a couple of streets away. So the interviews went something like this:

'Do you know James Smith?'

'Yes.'

'How did you know him?'

'Nothing further to say.'

'James has spoken to us and given us his version of events.'

'Sorry, I knew James when he worked as a mechanic at the garage where I was a spray painter.'

Then, just as suddenly, all further questions about Mr Smith were met with the usual response of 'no comment'.

Just as puzzling was Sinclair's willingness to talk about what for him must have been the most difficult subject of all – his sexuality and his relationships with various women. A series of exchanges saw him at once talk about matters right at the heart of the inquiry and then, in the next answer, refuse to answer fairly innocuous inquiries.

'Did you enjoy sex?'

'Yes, I did.'

Then, when asked if he had any preferences, Sinclair laughed as he said, 'No further comment to make.'

He claimed his first sexual relationship after coming out of jail at the end of his sentence for the killing of Catherine Reehill was with a woman in Edinburgh. He refused to say if he lived with her but did tell us that he got a sexually transmitted disease from her.

He would list the names of his wife's siblings but refuse to say which ones he was friendly with. This was perhaps more understandable as he had committed sexual crimes with one of them and crimes of violence with another.

When reminded, after another break, that the interview was really concerning the events surrounding the death of Anna Kenny, it was back to the 'no comment' replies and so the pattern continued – tiny revelations, followed by 'No comment.'

The officers asked if he had ever been to Argyll and he said he had but, when asked if he had been to Skipness, the scene of the disposal of Anna's body, it was back to the standard 'no comment' reply.

Then he came up with an answer to a question that rather bowled us over. Bear in mind that, over many hours of interviews, the only information that had been forthcoming was of a bland, non-incriminatory nature. Some of his answers shed a tiny bit of light into certain areas we were interested in but that was all. Maintaining concentration and direction over lengthy interviews like this can be demanding and it is all too easy for minds to begin to wander off. I don't know if Calum and Joe were at this stage – three hours or so into that day's session with Sinclair – but, if they had been, they were to snap back quickly. Once again they had reminded him he was being interviewed about the murder of Anna Kenny. A book of interview aids had maps, a picture of the caravanette, the dead girl and even one shot of the Hurdy Gurdy pub where she was last seen alive. Sinclair denied being in the pub at any time and took the opportunity of repeating that he was never much of a drinker. When shown a picture of the pub, he casually dropped into the conversation the fact that he had once been on the roof of the pub – only then it was a bookmaker's shop and Sinclair told the officers he was on the roof trying to break in. What was that all about? Did he think that we would be impressed by his candour about his visit to a building right at the heart of our inquiry? Or was it a distraction to try to establish that he had no fear of admitting his association with the place? Whatever the reason, his talkativeness soon passed and it was back to 'no comment'. He had no comment to make on Gordon Hamilton's wife, Wilma, except to say he didn't remember her. We knew of a violent row Sinclair had with Gordon the night before his marriage to Wilma which ended with neither Sinclair nor Sarah attending the wedding the next day. But this was getting too warm – it was an area much too central to Sinclair's killing spree – and he clammed up again as quickly as he had begun to speak.

Then, six hours into the interview which had only been punctuated with short breaks, the full facts of Anna Kenny's murder as we knew them were put to Sinclair. As usual, I was in a nearby room watching the interview with other senior officers as it took place. The tension building up in the interview room was clearly visible on our TV monitor as the officers summed up the case against him and offered him the opportunity to rebut the allegations one by one. As he declined to reply to the main allegations and sought to dismiss the lesser ones, Sinclair remained as calm and composed as he'd always been. He appeared cold and remote and the whole interview showed him in a particularly bad light but we needed more and we didn't have it.

Early in December, Sinclair was again interviewed at Govan police station. The usual recording and monitoring was in place. It was obvious he had realised that he had gone too far in previous sessions and, this time, he stuck rigidly to his 'no comment' plan.

Our tactics changed slightly to see if we could reach through to how we considered Sinclair perceived himself. We believed he thought of himself as two Angus Sinclairs. There was the bad one of all those years ago – wicked, violent and unreliable – and there was the new one, the good one, the one who was trusted, respected and liked by those around him. So Calum and Joe decided they would try to contact the good Sinclair to see if he might be willing to reveal details of the bad one.

This time, they painted a picture of the life of Hilda McAuley for him. They highlighted her hard-working nature and the love she had for her sons. A photograph of the three of them, mother and sons together and smiling, was produced – Hilda's love for her boys was clearly reciprocated. Calum told how, on the night of her murder, the children had helped their mum get ready to go out. They kissed her goodbye and never saw her again. They pointed out the similarities with his own family, even handing him a current photograph of his own son who he hadn't seen for many years.

Again and again, Sinclair refused to budge from his 'no comment' stance and the familiar scene of questions being asked and no answers given was played out. Whether it was frustration and anger or guilt I do not know but, during this interview, Sinclair seemed to retreat into himself. He no longer maintained eye contact with the officers and he sat, with his arms folded, staring down at the floor. It was as if he had built a defensive cocoon around himself.

At one point in this session, we allowed him a visit from his sister who had been as helpful as she could to us throughout the investigation. We do not know what exchanges took place between Sinclair and his sister but I believe she tried as hard as she could to persuade him to tell the whole truth for his sake and that of his entire family. It was to no avail and, when the interview continued, it was 'nothing further to say' all the way.

191

During all the interviews when he was asked about the deaths of Helen and Christine, Anna, Matilda and Agnes, Sinclair gave nothing away. Protected by his right of silence, we were met by his stony resistance – just as we had feared we would be. Clearly all his years of imprisonment had done nothing to soften him.

12

Trial

As the investigation progressed, we felt we were beginning to put together a convincing case. The evidence in the World's End case was strong despite the fact that one of our suspects, Gordon Hamilton, was dead. Angus Sinclair had been positively identified through DNA from samples taken from Helen and Christine and strong traces of Sinclair's DNA had also been found in the knots and bindings that had been used to secure the girls on that dark night in October 1977. We were very grateful for the diligence shown by our scientists in carefully preserving those items since they were recovered from the crime scenes all those years ago – had they not done so, we wouldn't have had our full DNA profile of Sinclair. In addition, we had compelling hairs and fibres evidence linking Helen to materials used in vehicles similar to the Toyota caravanette we knew Sinclair had been driving at the time but which was now beyond our reach. We also had expert opinion that suggested Helen and Christine had not been bound and gagged by the same individual – like so many other habits, knot-tying tends to follow distinctive personal patterns. We thought it was significant that the knots used on one of the girls were all perfectly symmetrical reef knots while all the knots used on the other body were grannies which suggested a more haphazard approach. When we had considered this aspect of the case, our minds went back to Angus Sinclair's early prison training at Aberdeen, fishing net repair, where consistent and uniform knot tying was essential and would have become second nature to a man working in the repair of nets for so long. Lastly, we could prove Sinclair's connections with the area of the World's End pub and we had traced one of Sinclair's ex-girlfriends who told us they had visited East Lothian near the deposition sites. Given the passage of time, it was as much as we could have hoped for.

In the Glasgow killings, we lacking the kind of forensic evidence we had in the World's End murders but, nonetheless, the Strathclyde team had built a good case of circumstantial evidence which, when taken together with what we had for the World's End case, would, we felt, present a strong case to a jury.

The evidence that we could not, of course, present was that Sinclair had killed and raped before. We couldn't say that the use of Mary Gallagher's trousers as a ligature bore striking similarities to all our cases. In England and Wales, evidence of 'similar fact' – that is the accused has been proven to act in this way before – is admissible and has been crucial in a number of notable cases. In Scotland, such evidence is not admissible. Sinclair would, therefore, eventually appear in court as an innocent man with the jury having no knowledge of his background. This aspect of Scots law is to preserve fairness to the accused and dates, as do so many other fundamentals of the law, to a time when capital punishment meant that there were lives at stake. Nowadays, many of us who have worked in the criminal justice system would view it as a little archaic – the inability to present such evidence has, in my view, meant that the balance of fairness has swung very much in favour of the accused and away from the victim and public interest.

However, those are the rules of the system and we knew we had to work within them. As our investigation concluded, we drew up a comprehensive report and submitted it to the Crown Office. It is the job of the Crown Office to decide on prosecution, settle the nature of the charges and then take the case forward to trial.

Many people imagine this is a straightforward, clinical process –

that the handing over of the report ends police involvement and begins the prosecution phase. In minor cases it is but in major cases it is far more complicated than that. In serious or complex cases, a senior procurator fiscal will take an interest from an early stage, sometimes directing lines of inquiry, but usually monitoring the development of the case. At the stage where it becomes apparent that there is a reasonable body of evidence and that the case is probably destined for the High Court, an advocate-depute is appointed to lead the case for the Crown and to keep abreast of the inquiry. The advocate-depute's role is crucial for he or she will ultimately recommend to the Crown Office exactly what charges should appear on the indictment. Then, with the senior procurator fiscal, the advocate-depute prepares the case for court and leads the prosecution when the case finally appears in the High Court. Some may see this as a blurring of the lines between police and prosecution but, in fact, it usually works well with each party being very aware of their own role and remit.

From early in Operation Trinity, we had been in detailed consultation with a senior procurator fiscal and, well before our investigations were complete, an advocate-depute had been appointed to lead the prosecution both in its preparation and through to the eventual trial. We were fortunate that the advocate-depute we had was one of the rising stars in the Crown Office and he quickly got to grips with the complexities of the five cases. This was no easy task – we had been living with the cases for months and, in some cases, years but the advocate-depute would be starting from scratch.

One of the early decisions he had to make was what should appear on the indictment – in other words, precisely what charges should eventually be brought against Angus Sinclair. During the ten months of our joint investigation, we had amassed a mountain of evidence not just relating to the murders but to a number of other serious violent and sexual crimes all committed in the late 70s, prior to Sinclair's arrest for the sex attacks on the girls in Glasgow. The crimes we had uncovered were all serious and if they had been current, they would have been prosecuted with vigour. As it was the passage of time, almost thirty years, meant that their importance had faded. The decision was taken that it was not in the public interest to prosecute Sinclair for those crimes given the length of time that had elapsed.

We fully understood and half expected this decision but, none-theless, it carried risks. On the one hand, you could see how it would look from the Crown Office's point of view. It could be hazardous to clutter the indictment with less serious crimes when the major issue was the five murders. On the other hand, we felt that these more minor offences painted a background to Sinclair's behaviour and pattern of offending and there were living witnesses who could have described what happened to the jury. It may have been compelling evidence but ultimately we accepted it was the Crown Office's and the advocate-depute's decision. He was a very able man and he was the one who would be presenting the case in court so we respected his judgement.

That left the five murders. The Edinburgh World's End case of Helen and Christine, together with the Glasgow cases of Anna Kenny, Hilda McAuley and Agnes Cooney.

By this time, the prosecuting team was comprised of the advocate-depute and a senior procurator fiscal from Glasgow who had replaced the Edinburgh procurator fiscal to ensure a geographical spread of responsibility – although, as a safeguard, a senior procurator fiscal in Edinburgh retained an interest. It seemed a reasonable idea at the time but later, as things developed, it would prove to be the source of some difficulty.

We always knew the viability of the five cases depended on the strength of the evidence in the World's End case. We hoped that together they would stand up in court but accepted that, separately, the Glasgow cases still lacked sufficient evidence. The critical decision had to be made – would they stand together or would the weakness of the Glasgow cases threaten the World's End case? Although the Crown Office and the police had had fairly close consultations throughout, we knew that this was a decision they and the advocate-depute would make alone.

Eventually, in spring 2005, the Crown Office decided not to proceed with the Glasgow cases but to serve an indictment on Angus Sinclair charging him with the World's End murders of Helen Scott and Christine Eadie. It was a disappointment for us all but the bitterest of blows for Eddie McCusker and his team from Strathclyde. It was Eddie's last major investigation and he had worked tirelessly to build a case – no one could have done more – but the Crown Office's decision was absolute and final.

There was only one advantage and that was that the strength of the World's End case could not now be jeopardised by weaker cases. Even so, the underlying feeling was one of disappointment. We were convinced we had the right man but the thirty-year gap and the lack of forensic evidence in the Glasgow cases meant that, despite our best efforts, we would never be able to prove it.

So, after all, we were left with the World's End cases. It wasn't the end result Operation Trinity had been working towards but, in Lothian and Borders, it remained of prime importance and we were confident that we had a very strong case.

As the preparations went ahead, the defence team were given full access to all the documents and papers we'd accumulated over the years. The rules of full disclosure, obligatory in England and Wales, have gradually been accepted as routine in Scotland. This means that the defence has the right to see any evidence we had gathered which offers them an excellent opportunity to pick holes in an inquiry, especially a historic one like this. It took the defence team a year to review all the evidence but, apart from the delay in going to trial caused by this, we had few worries. We were confident that all the evidence and documents in the World's End case had been properly and professionally cared for over the years. There were flaws but they were minor and understandable in the circumstances.

Eventually the defence had done their preparation and a slot of six weeks was estimated by the Crown Office team as being required for the trial. This was an important decision. High Court time is scarce – the courts are overloaded with work – but it was calculated that, to lead the weight of the prosecution evidence and to accommodate the defence, a trial of six weeks would be needed.

But things were beginning to change. In October 2006, the advocate-depute who had been so actively involved with the case for months and who had carefully led the preparations for the trial was promoted and the responsibility was passed to a new advocate-depute. At the same time, the lead procurator fiscal who had been retained in the Edinburgh office, an able and highly respected individual, was also on the move leaving the original lead fiscal based in Glasgow but, by now, responsible for the Edinburgh cases of the World's End murders alone – crimes that were not geo-graphically the responsibility of the Glasgow fiscal's area and of which there was no deep-seated knowledge or ownership. This may seem insignificant but there were also practical difficulties as documents had to be ferried back and forward across the country and the lines of communication were extended.

While the various moves in staff were all unconnected to the case, we were dismayed by the changes. The senior and well-regarded prosecutors who had been involved throughout the investigation – the ones who had made the key decisions and had planned the Crown Office case – would not be in court or play any part in the trial after all.

Worryingly for us, there also seemed to be a rejection or at least a strong doubt in the minds of the prosecution team about the low copy number DNA evidence that forensic experts from England had identified in the knots of the ligatures used to bind Helen and Christine. This evidence did not provide a complete profile of Sinclair but did offer a partial one – an indication which we believed would have been compelling to a jury. We knew that low copy number DNA profiling was controversial and the forensic science community was divided as to its worth. We were also aware that, in the background, an Australian case involving the murder of a British man, Peter Falconio, was adding to the controversy over reliability of low copy number DNA profiling. Nonetheless, we felt that if this evidence was carefully presented, it would offer strong support to our case because the low copy number DNA traces and the different methods of tying the knots pointed to two people being involved in the binding and gagging with a very strong pointer to Sinclair as being one of them.

Ultimately, the Crown Office decided not to lead this evidence, thereby excluding expert evidence of a high quality and leaving the case strong but one-dimensional. In the end, this proved fatal when Sinclair's legal team, at late notice, changed their defence to consensual contact – thus dealing a blow to the single-strand Crown Office case.

By this time, Ian Thomas, Eddie McCusker and I had retired from the police service and Allan Jones had taken responsibility for the police component of the trial. Not that this was of any concern – no one knew more or was better placed to handle the final stages of the police case than Allan. In hindsight, however, I regret that Ian Thomas and I left when we did. However, we had no choice – our police service was completed and we had other commitments. I had already stayed on for eight months past my planned retiring date but it left the case light of senior police champions. Ian Thomas and I could only look on anxiously as things started to unravel.

There had been too many changes – a new advocate-depute, a lead procurator fiscal who was remote geographically and the rejection of a considerable body of supporting evidence. Separately these issues were concerning but, when put together, they were deeply worrying those close to the case.

Eventually, over three years after we reopened the case, the trial of Angus Sinclair opened on Monday, 27 August 2007, just six weeks short of the thirtieth anniversary of the World's End murders. In the new court building, next to the Crown Office in Chambers Street, Edinburgh, not a mile from the World's End pub, he was at last called to account for the murders of Helen Scott and Christine Eadie.

As the date of the trial approached, the liaison between the Crown Office team and the lead officers had been maintained but it came as a shock when, on the opening day, the advocate-depute made it known that he intended to cut the trial short – from the six weeks originally estimated by the Crown Office to only two. This was of real concern to many of us connected to the case – we knew the bulk and the weight of evidence that still remained and we struggled to imagine how the case could be cut to two weeks without important material having to be excluded. It was, however, a tactical decision which was the Crown Office's to make. We were worried but we just had to live with it.

As the trial drew near, we had speculated as to what Sinclair's tactics would be – his defence had, after all, had over a year to consider their approach. They had also had complete access to all the data, old and new, from the thirty-year inquiry. It seemed to us that Sinclair had three options. The first, pleading guilty on the day, was out of the question. It wasn't in his nature and, in any event, he had nothing to lose by playing it long – after all, he was going nowhere and his expensive legal team was not costing him a penny. The second and more likely option was that he offered no defence but let the Crown Office prove its case. He had tried this unsuccessfully in the Mary Gallagher case but it was still worth a try – thirty years is a long time and his lawyers might have picked some loophole in the continuity of evidence that could cast sufficient doubt on the case against him.

In the event, he chose the route we thought he would – he blamed his conveniently dead brother-in-law, Gordon Hamilton, in the special defence of impeachment and furthermore claimed that any trace of his DNA on the bodies of Helen and Christine was as a result of consensual sex. It was always his best chance – everyone he blamed or alleged to be complicit was dead. Gordon Hamilton could not give his version of events and poor Helen and Christine, just seventeen years old when they died, were not there to rebut his hateful suggestion that they had willingly had sex with him.

As we've seen, he had the advantage of no one knowing about his awful past – the jury had no inkling of the dozen rape victims or the two other girls proven to have died at his hands. But it was also a risky strategy for, in impeaching his dead brother-in-law and claiming consensual sex with the two young girls, he was placing himself at the scene of the crimes. He had sought to neutralise the power of the DNA evidence but, in doing so, he had implicated himself. This approach also made him potentially vulnerable in other areas. How could he explain his denials and the long silences during the many hours of interviews and then suddenly offer this defence? And it would look odd if he decided not to give evidence himself – after all, an innocent man would surely welcome the chance to deny such awful allegations personally. But, if he did give evidence and forgo his right to silence, he was taking the most awful risk. If he entered the witness box in the High Court, he would have to subject himself to a rigorous examination by the prosecuting advocate-depute. His usual tactics of sullen silence would not work in the High Court. It was something he had never dared to do before. In all his many court appearances, in all his interviews, he had always hidden behind his right to silence. In the event, he didn't have to face these challenges – the jury never got the chance to make a judgement on the character and behaviour of Angus Sinclair.

The defence of consensual sex also laid bare the flaw in the Crown Office's approach to the low-copy DNA evidence which would have been powerful in rebutting the suggestion of consent.

We had evidence of materials from inside the knots used in tying the girls up that revealed a partial profile of Sinclair's DNA. In one particular sample, a DNA band unique to Sinclair – that is to say one that was not shared by Hamilton, Helen or Christine – was identified. Our experts had calculated a 1 in 390 probability of finding one of those bands elsewhere in the UK's population. This may not seem a lot but, given Sinclair's admission that he was there, it actually significantly strengthened that probability.

The low-copy evidence together with the expert witnesses we had who were willing to interpret the knot tying would have done much to rebut the claim of consent and, when it was made known to us what Sinclair's defence would be, we hoped the Crown Office would reconsider their decision not to present these strands of evidence and would seek to introduce them. In the event, they did not and nor was the evidence of a timeline introduced. This meant there was a potential gap in the understanding of judge and jury about the likely time of death of Helen and Christine. This led the judge to conclude that the girls could have been killed at any time up until the discovery of their bodies – some fifteen to nineteen hours after they were last seen. In fact, we had evidence from pathologists to show that the girls died shortly after they were last seen. Had this evidence been introduced, it would have been harder for Sinclair to credibly claim consensual sexual contact and yet distance himself from the murders.

The disastrous consequences of these omissions would shortly become apparent as the trial of *Her Majesty's Advocate* v *Sinclair* began.

As in every murder trial, the case started slowly – there was some scene setting and time devoted to proving the crime had been committed. The friends who last saw the girls alive came through the court giving their thirty-year-old recollections. It was a strange experience. Having read their statements so many times, we felt we knew them personally but, of course, for us, they were frozen in time, back in 1977. It was odd to see the teenage pals of Helen and Christine stand in the box as middle-aged men and women. Then came the witnesses who'd found the bodies, followed by the first police officers on the scenes – these officers were all now long retired, some for over twenty years.

The defence's tactics became clear – the prosecution's case depended on the DNA evidence and, regardless of Sinclair's claim of consensual sex, there were other considerations. DNA is susceptible to contamination and, back in the 70s, this had not been a consideration so could there not have been some cross-contamination? After all, no protective clothing or face masks were used in these days. It was all designed to create a haze of doubt in the minds of the jury and it would be hammered home by the defence even if the claim of consensual sex was rejected – thirty years was a long time, witnesses' memories were vague, systems were different, mistakes may have been made, there may be room for doubt and there could be no room for doubt to convict. The standard of proof is clear and set high – to convict, the jury must be sure of guilt beyond all reasonable doubt. And, in any case, the slight, elderly man in the dock had given an explanation and, as unlikely as it seemed, the Crown Office's case was not structured in a way to attack it.

One of the saddest elements of any murder trial is when the family and friends give evidence and try to describe in words the events that shattered their lives and marked them for ever. Morain Scott and Christine's mother, Margaret, spoke of their daughters and gave an account of their last days and the night they left their homes never to return. Both spoke of the impact that the events of October 1977 had on their lives. Then the court heard how Helen's mother had never recovered from her daughter's death and had quickly declined into ill-health and died prematurely. They were not in the witness box long and there were no startling revelations as they went through their evidence but the feeling of despair was tangible.

No words could come close to describing the injury done to the Scott and Eadie families.

The remaining course of the trial was nondescript and brief. Amazingly, the special defence and the claim of consensual sex were seen to neutralise the DNA evidence. This we found unbelievable. Two young women had been found gagged, bound, raped and murdered and the man whose semen is found in them lodges an implausible defence of consent which is accepted without question. It frankly beggared belief.

As the thin list of Crown Office's witnesses came to an end, there was an awful feeling of anticlimax. We had put together a strong case but you wouldn't have known it from the lacklustre presentation in court. Then the final blow fell. We learned that the defence were going to motion for no case to answer. It was beyond belief. How could a man whose semen was found in two murdered girls have no case to answer? It defied all logic and it challenged common sense but it succeeded. The judge agreed the defence's motion before a shocked court. The advocate-depute was not in the court and nor was the lead procurator fiscal, who had been largely absent throughout the trial. The trial had ended and there was no right for the Crown to appeal

All connected to the case felt the blow. Experienced court journalists had never seen the like and, on the jury benches, there was amazement. Looking at their faces, I doubted if any of this group of ordinary citizens had been fooled by Angus Robertson Sinclair.

The prosecution handling of the case was, at first sight, inexplicable. Why had so much evidence been left out? When considered on cool reflection it was, however, all too easy to see what had gone wrong. As usual, there was no single glaring error – just a series of small events, changes in personnel, questionable decisions over evidence that all combined to weaken the case that went to court. The decision had been taken to strip the case bare and lead on the powerful primary DNA evidence. The theory may have been to keep it simple and that to do otherwise would confuse the jury. In the event, the single pillar of the prosecution case was brittle and was effectively neutralised by Sinclair's special defence. He never had to explain himself or justify his outrageous claims of consensual sex with Helen and Christine. The law protected him from that.

Outside the court Helen's father, Morain Scott, composed to the last and carrying himself with the same dignity as he had for thirty years, spoke for us all: 'The law it may have been – justice it was not.'

In the aftermath, the legal profession closed ranks but the damage had been done.

There were questions in Parliament and the media covered all aspects of the case and the trial extensively. The casual observer with an ounce of common sense could see that the outcome of the trial had been a terrible miscarriage of justice yet the usually voluble civil libertarians were silent. It seemed their concern for injustice only extended to accused persons, not victims.

And there was another casualty – the reputation of the Scottish justice system had taken a severe blow.

While there was the predictable defence of the judicial system, I believe the failure of the trial would be keenly felt at the Crown Office as well. The serving senior law officers in Scotland are of high quality, and behind the façade I feel sure they were as disappointed as us.

As I write, the Scottish Law Commission has recommended that the Crown be allowed to appeal against 'No case to answer' rulings. in serious cases. It is an important and positive development. Perhaps after all some good may come from 'The World's End.'

Conclusion

Setting aside the failure of the trial, what could we have done better and what lessons can we learn?

Looking back, it's always easy to criticise and to highlight where others have failed or could have done better – unfortunately it is a speciality of many sections of society today. In 1977, it was quite different and, reading through the old press cuttings, it's clear there was no attempt to find fault with the police investigation and nor was there intrusion, interference or the kind of wild speculation we see in prominent cases today. Instead the investigation was given a high profile, concern was expressed, every attempt to assist the investigation was made and warnings were issued to the public. We have come a long way since 1977 and it has not all been progress.

Of course things could have worked out better but that's not to say they could have been done better. We did not resolve the World's End case by traditional policing methods – we didn't come close. But, in fairness, it's hard to see what else the original team could have done. They followed the leads they had, they kept an ongoing and positive dialogue with Helen and Christine's parents – something that wasn't very common back then – and, most importantly, they stored and retained all the relevant documents and forensic evidence so that, thirty years later, we could capitalise on them. And, over the years, they appointed good officers to look after the case – officers who eventually, with the scientists, reached a conclusion. But there were flaws and some bad practice. The same

Identification Branch staff visited both sites and the bodies of both Helen and Christine were taken to the police mortuary in the same van. At the time this would not have appeared significant but, in the modern day, it would be deemed poor crime-scene management which the defence would highlight during the trial.

The first pathological examinations were also inconsistent, with small errors at both original post-mortems. These too would have consequences as they cast doubt on exact time of death which, thirty years later at the trial, became a factor.

The first phase of the investigation, in hindsight, concentrated on the crimes as local and committed massive resources to local inquiries. The systematic scanning of other crimes in other parts of the country was not prioritised or done thoroughly enough.

Undoubtedly the inter-force conference, when the heads of CID for East and West Scotland met in 1980, missed an opportunity to link cases earlier than they were but, accepting that, it is doubtful what benefit this would have brought given the lack of adequate administrative systems at the time. The consequential muddle may have been damaging to all. However, a link between the teams at that time may have seen to it that all the forensic productions were held in one safe and secure place and this could have prevented the loss or destruction of the forensic productions in the Glasgow cases. The absence of the forensic productions was a disaster for the Glasgow cases for it denied these investigations the enormous benefit of 21-century science that was to be the key to the progress of the World's End inquiry.

Should we have identified Angus Sinclair earlier, prevented some of his offences or been able to track down Gordon Hamilton in his lifetime? Sinclair was not a suspect or even on the database of the World's End case or any of the others. This is no surprise – he was relatively unknown in the late 1970s and the reputation he did have was for crimes of violence and dishonesty, his juvenile convictions having been largely forgotten. Crucially, he had no known connection with the areas of the World's End or East Lothian. But we still might have got on his trail earlier than we did.

We failed to fully understand the 1997 DNA breakthrough. This was partly the fault of the scientists for not explaining it to us properly and partly our ignorance of the new science. In the 1997 results, there was an indication of the presence of two men. Had we been aware of that, further examination may have identified Sinclair a full seven years earlier. This would not have prevented murder as Sinclair was already in prison but we would have been on the trail earlier – although, crucially, not during the lifetime of Gordon Hamilton.

But the best opportunity to identify links was in 2001 when Sinclair was arrested for the 1970s murder of Mary Gallagher. At that time, a connection could have been made with Mary's murder and the other outstanding cases both in Glasgow and Edinburgh. If a connection was made – and it's clear members of that team did suspect Sinclair of other offences – then it was not acted on or passed on and it was only when the National Crime and Operations Faculty did their analysis some years later that the links were made. Before that, there was no clear opportunity. After release from prison for the murder of Catherine Reehill, Sinclair's next serious conviction was for the rapes and assaults on the young girls in the early 80s. These offences were very different in profile from the murders so could not reasonably have been connected. In any event, the murders, both in Edinburgh and Glasgow, took place over a very short period during 1977 and 1978. No others were committed after Sinclair's offending pattern changed and consequently no lives could have been saved even if Sinclair had been identified at the earliest opportunity when he came to police notice in 1980.

Has Angus Sinclair escaped justice for other serious offences? Probably, but we will never know for certain. It is cold comfort but the families of the other murder victims from 1977 can take some consolation from the fact that, regardless of what the final tally of his convictions might be, Sinclair will end his days in prison where I believe he belongs.

But, if we are to learn lessons and use them to take us forward, then we should recognise that the lost opportunities point to a weakness in the way we investigated murders in the 1970s and, to some extent, still do. Murder is still seen as a local crime, a solution is sought locally and ownership of the case is tightly held locally. The statistics justify this approach. The vast majority of murders are of course local. The problems come with the few that are not and there can be even bigger problems when an offender ranges across different forces' areas committing crimes. The National Crime and Operations Faculty was established to cope with just such cases. The Faculty was of immense help to us during our investigation – its wide network of expertise and experience brought huge dividends as we picked our way through a complex investigation. Most importantly, it afforded us a connection with the foremost forensic scientists in the land who gave vital cutting-edge know-how that, in the end, made all the difference.

But even with the assistance of the Faculty, there remains the problem of how smaller police forces investigate large-scale or long-running murders. Smaller forces simply do not have the experienced investigators capable of conducting such inquiries. And nor can local forensic laboratories have the costly equipment or the staff expertise to carry out the complex procedures necessary in cases like the World's End. The newly formed Common Police Services arrangement and the Scottish Forensic Science Service with its centres of excellence should go a long way to resolve the forensic science issue, but the time must surely come when a truly national approach is taken to both current complex murder investigations and cold case inquiries where specialist skills are required. As the Scottish Police Service develops its Common Police Services, the way murder and other serious crimes are investigated and supported must surely be reviewed and enhanced.

Conclusion

But the most intriguing question for the investigators today is to decide how far and in what direction forensic evidence will develop in the future. The World's End murders were resolved when forensic science developed to the extent that it could extract vital evidence from materials which had been of no evidential value in the 1970s. The crucial question is what materials, so far deemed worthless, will reveal vital evidence in the future? What do we retain, how and where? We cannot keep it all but, if we calculate that forensic science will continue to develop in the way it has over the last thirty years, then we must make sure we are best placed to take advantage of its advances. It is an exercise in futurology to be sure but the advantages could be significant.

Finally, what are we to conclude from the World's End murders and the case of Angus Sinclair? The trial was a disaster for all the reasons I have described in the last chapter but even if he had been convicted it would have made no difference, other than the satisfaction of seeing justice done and bringing some closure for the Scott and Eadie families. Whatever the outcome, Helen and Christine are still dead and Angus Sinclair is still in prison. Regardless of the result, this case could never have been cast as a triumph – too many people are dead and damaged for that. Let us not forget that the murder of Helen and Christine, the deaths of Anna, Matilda and Agnes, were disasters not only for the young women themselves but for their families on down the generations. There was never going to be cause for celebration.

Furthermore, the observer cannot avoid the inescapable conclusion that society and the justice system failed Helen Scott, Christine Eadie and their families twice and failed them badly. Apart from the trial, the truth is that we always knew how dangerous Angus Sinclair was – he was assessed with pinpoint accuracy after he killed Catherine Reehill in the 1960s – yet he was released to kill, rape and brutalise again and again.

Much, of course, has changed in thirty years but I wonder to what extent. With pressure on prison places, how many young Angus Sinclairs are even today being processed towards liberty despite the assessment of professionals and while they are still a danger to the public.

This is not an easy matter – decisions must be made and some risks taken – but, in the aftermath of the World's End murders, the question of how different things might have been had Sinclair's early assessments been fully considered gives food for thought.

Of course, the crimes which I describe here happened a long time ago. In today's immediate and fast-moving world, reflecting on the policing of the 1970s is almost like the study of ancient history. Yet, for some, the events of 1977 are as fresh today as they were on the day their world changed for ever. For the families and friends of the victims, Helen, Christine, Anna, Matilda, Agnes and all the others, there is no respite and there never will be – only the raw, open wound of grief month on month, year on year. In fairness, victims do get much better treatment than they used to. Family liaison officers, victim impact statements and most of all the incredible work done by the trained volunteers of the Victim Support Service – they have all made a difference. Yet I am sure it is not enough and we must go further. It is said that the mark of a civilised society is the way it treats its prisoners. If this is true, then it is surely the mark of a compassionate, right-minded society that victims are treated just as well, if not better. In our current obsession with human rights, this is all too often not the case. I do not argue with the need for effective rehabilitation of prisoners – quite the reverse and not from any liberal sense of goodness. We must make the best efforts at rehabilitation for all the practical reasons – and most of all to try to curtail reoffending. But I hope that we also continue to drive for better treatment of victims and a recognition that there are primary and secondary victims and that the victims' families in serious crimes deserve respect, consideration and support.

Conclusion

Fortunately, I have never been a victim of serious crime and nor have any of my family or friends been seriously injured by any criminal act of others, but I have rubbed up against too many victims not to feel their anguish.

I hope that, in future, victims' services are expanded and their funding secured and enhanced – not for tea and sympathy but to offer ongoing information and advice. We must make sure that victims' voices are heard even from beyond the grave and that they are given the respect they deserve. Most importantly, we need to properly consider the continuing needs of victims, both primary and secondary, in the wider context.

It has always intrigued and perplexed me that offenders' programmes are so much more numerous and better funded than our victims' services. I believe it is time that the balance changed.

This book is written in memory of Helen and Christine – and Anna, Matilda and Agnes – but it is dedicated to the other victims, the ones we tend to overlook and forget in time, the families and the friends who have lost. They will never forget and we should not forget them.

Finally, it would be wrong not to conclude by saluting the generations of police officers, scientists and support staff who brought the World's End case to a close, especially those who stood the lonely watches, through the long and fruitless years, and who never gave up, who never stopped trying, never stood aside and who finally by dedication and willpower succeeded.

They represent all that is best in the Scottish Police Service. It was an honour to work with them.